15 Best President Obama Speeches

Transcripts in his own words

ISBN: 9781686803338

CONTENTS

INTRODUCTION
15 Best President Obama Speeches

How can anyone choose the best of anything?
It should probably be called "Greatest Speeches" but
I don't think anyone searches for that term, and I
wanted this to be found.

I spent a few months researching articles on the best
speeches in the eyes of President Barack Obama's
White House staffers, speechwriters, and those who
witnessed them.

It was a delicious break from scrolling through
petulant tweets and social media nonsense, and a
process which created this selection of 15 speeches.

What is certain is that anyone choosing would pick a
different 15, so if there are any undeserving choices,
why not send a petulant tweet with the hashtag
#ObamaSpeeches

The list is presented in chronological order and tells
its own story, although dipping in at random has its
own surprises.

Where possible, transcripts of the speeches are
presented as delivered in public rather than as
written.

Thanks for coming along on this journey.

August 2019

1 "Let's face it, my presence on this stage is pretty unlikely"

Democratic National Convention Keynote Address
July 27, 2004
Fleet Center, Boston, Massachusetts

The keynote address at the 2004 Democratic National Convention (DNC) given by Illinois State Senator, United States senatorial candidate, and future President Barack Obama in Boston, Massachusetts. His unexpected landslide victory in the March 2004 Illinois U.S. Senate Democratic primary made him a rising star within the national Democratic Party overnight, started speculation about a presidential future, and led to the reissue of his memoir, Dreams from My Father.

On behalf of the great state of Illinois, crossroads of a nation, land of Lincoln, let me express my deep gratitude for the privilege of addressing this convention. Tonight is a particular honor for me because, let's face it, my presence on this stage is pretty unlikely.

My father was a foreign student, born and raised in a small village in Kenya. He grew up herding goats, went to school in a tin-roof shack. His father, my grandfather, was a cook, a domestic servant to the British.

But my grandfather had larger dreams for his son. Through hard work and perseverance my father got a scholarship to study in a magical place; America, that shone as a beacon of freedom and opportunity to so many who had come before. While studying here, my father met my mother. She was born in a town on the other side of the world, in Kansas. Her father worked on oil rigs and farms through most of the Depression.

The day after Pearl Harbor my grandfather signed up for duty, joined Patton's army, marched across Europe. Back home, my grandmother raised a baby and went to work on a bomber assembly line. After the war, they studied on the GI Bill, bought a house through FHA, and later moved west - all the way to Hawaii - in search of opportunity.

And they, too, had big dreams for their daughter. A common dream, born of two continents. My parents shared not only an improbable love; they shared an abiding faith in the possibilities of this nation.

They would give me an African name, Barack, or "blessed," believing that in a tolerant America your name is no barrier to success. They imagined me going to the best schools in the land, even though they weren't rich, because in a generous America you don't have to be rich to achieve your potential. They are both passed away now. And yet, I know that on this night, they look down on me with great pride.

They stand here and I stand here today, grateful for the diversity of my heritage, aware that my parents' dreams live on in my two precious daughters. I stand here knowing that my story is part of the larger American story, that I owe a debt to all of those who came before me, and that in no other country on earth is my story even possible.

Tonight, we gather to affirm the greatness of our nation, not because of the height of our skyscrapers, or the power of our military, or the size of our economy. Our pride is based on a very simple premise, summed up in a declaration made over two hundred years ago, "We hold these truths to be self-evident, that all men are created equal. That they are endowed by their Creator with certain inalienable rights. That among these are life, liberty and the pursuit of happiness."

That is the true genius of America, a faith in simple dreams, an insistence on small miracles.

That we can tuck in our children at night and know that they are fed and clothed and safe from harm.

That we can say what we think, write what we think, without hearing a sudden knock on the door.

That we can have an idea and start our own business without paying a bribe.

That we can participate in the political process without fear of retribution, and that our votes will be counted - at least most of the time.

This year, in this election, we are called to reaffirm our values and our commitments, to hold them against a hard reality and see how we are measuring up, to the legacy of our forbearers, and the promise of future generations. And fellow Americans - Democrats, Republicans, Independents - I say to you tonight: we have more work to do. More work to do for the workers I met in Galesburg, Illinois, who are losing their union jobs at the Maytag plant that's moving to Mexico, and now are having to compete with their own children for jobs that pay seven bucks an hour. More to do for the father that I met who was losing his job and choking back the tears, wondering how he would pay $4,500 a month for the drugs his son needs without the health benefits that he counted on. More to do for the young woman in East St. Louis, and thousands more like her, who has the grades, has the drive, has the will, but doesn't have the money to go to college.

Now don't get me wrong. The people I meet in small towns and big cities, in diners and office parks, they don't expect government to solve all their problems.

They know they have to work hard to get ahead and they want to. Go into the collar counties around Chicago, and people will tell you they don't want their tax money wasted by a welfare agency or by the Pentagon. Go into any inner city neighborhood, and folks will tell you that government alone can't teach our kids to learn. They know that parents have to teach, that children can't achieve unless we raise their expectations and turn off the television sets and eradicate the slander that says a black youth with a book is acting white. They know those things. People don't expect government to solve all their problems.

But they sense, deep in their bones, that with just a slight change in priorities, we can make sure that every child in America has a decent shot at life, and that the doors of opportunity remain open to all. They know we can do better. And they want that choice.

In this election, we offer that choice. Our party has chosen a man to lead us who embodies the best this country has to offer, and that man is John Kerry. John Kerry understands the ideals of community, faith, and service, because they've defined his life. From his heroic service [in] Vietnam to his years as prosecutor and lieutenant governor, through two decades in the United States Senate, he has devoted himself to this country. Again and again, we've seen him make tough choices when easier ones were available. His values and his record affirm what is best in us.

John Kerry believes in an America where hard work is rewarded. So instead of offering tax breaks to companies shipping jobs overseas, he offers them to companies creating jobs here at home. John Kerry believes in an America where all Americans can afford the same health coverage our politicians in Washington have for themselves. John Kerry believes in energy independence, so we aren't held hostage to the profits of oil companies or the sabotage of foreign oil fields. John Kerry believes in the constitutional freedoms that have made our country the envy of the world, and he will never sacrifice our basic liberties nor use faith as a wedge to divide us. And John Kerry believes that in a dangerous world, war must be an option sometimes, but it should never be the first option.

You know a while back I met a young man named Shamus in a VFW Hall in East Moline, Illinois. He was a good-looking kid, six-two, six-three, clear eyed, with an easy smile. He told me he'd joined the Marines and was heading to Iraq the following week. And as I listened to him explain why he'd enlisted, the absolute faith he had in our country and its leaders, his devotion to duty and service, I thought this young man was all that any of us might ever hope for in a child.

But then I asked myself: Are we serving Shamus as well as he's serving us? I thought of the 900 men and women, sons and daughters, husbands and wives, friends and neighbors, who won't be returning to their own hometowns. I thought of families I had met who were struggling to get by without a loved one's full income, or whose loved ones had returned with a limb missing or nerves shattered, but still lacked long-term health benefits because they were reservists.

When we send our young men and women into harm's way, we have a solemn obligation not to fudge the numbers or shade the truth about why they're going, to care for their families while they're gone, to tend to the soldiers upon their return, and to never ever go to war without enough troops to win the war, secure the peace, and earn the respect of the world.

Now let me be clear. We have real enemies in the world. These enemies must be found. They must be pursued and they must be defeated. John Kerry knows this. And just as Lieutenant Kerry did not hesitate to risk his life to protect the men who served with him in Vietnam, President Kerry will not hesitate one moment to use our military might to keep America safe and secure. John Kerry believes in America. And he knows that it's not enough for just some of us to prosper. For alongside our famous individualism, there's another ingredient in the American saga.

A belief that we're all connected as one people. If there's a child on the south side of Chicago who can't read, that matters to me, even if it's not my child. If there's a senior citizen somewhere who can't pay for their prescription drugs and having to choose between medicine and the rent, that makes my life poorer, even if it's not my grandparent.

If there's an Arab American family being rounded up without benefit of an attorney or due process, that threatens my civil liberties. It is that fundamental belief - I am my brother's keeper, I am my sister's keeper that makes this country work. It's what allows us to pursue our individual dreams, and yet still come together as one American family.
"E pluribus unum." Out of many, one.

Now even as we speak, there are those who are preparing to divide us, the spin masters, the negative ad peddlers who embrace the politics of anything goes. Well, I say to them tonight, there is not a liberal America and a conservative America--there is the United States of America. There is not a black America and white America and Latino America and Asian America; there is the United States of America.

The pundits like to slice-and-dice our country into Red States and Blue States; Red States for Republicans, Blue States for Democrats. But I've got news for them, too. We worship an awesome God in the Blue States, and we don't like federal agents poking around in our libraries in the Red States. We coach Little League in the Blue States, and yes we've got some gay friends in the Red States. There are patriots who opposed the war in Iraq and there are patriots who supported the war in Iraq. We are one people, all of us pledging allegiance to the stars and stripes, all of us defending the United States of America.

In the end, that's what this election is about. Do we participate in a politics of cynicism or do we participate in a politics of hope? John Kerry calls on us to hope. John Edwards calls on us to hope. I'm not talking about blind optimism here. The almost willful ignorance that thinks unemployment will go away if we just don't think about it, or the health care crisis will solve itself if we just ignore it. That's not what I'm talking about.

I'm talking about something more substantial. It's the hope of slaves sitting around a fire singing freedom songs; the hope of immigrants setting out for distant shores; the hope of a young naval lieutenant bravely patrolling the Mekong Delta; the hope of a millworker's son who dares to defy the odds; the hope of a skinny kid with a funny name who believes that America has a place for him, too. Hope in the face of difficulty. Hope in the face of uncertainty. The audacity of hope!

In the end, that is God's greatest gift to us, the bedrock of this nation; a belief in things not seen; a belief that there are better days ahead.

I believe that we can give our middle class relief and provide working families with a road to opportunity. I believe we can provide jobs to the jobless, homes to the homeless, and reclaim young people in cities across America from violence and despair. I believe that we have a righteous wind at our backs and that as we stand on the crossroads of history, we can make the right choices, and meet the challenges that face us.

America, tonight, if you feel the same energy that I do, if you feel the same urgency that I do, if you feel the same passion that I do, if you feel the same hopefulness that I do - if we do what we must do, then I have no doubt that all across the country, from Florida to Oregon, from Washington to Maine, the people will rise up in November, and John Kerry will be sworn in as president, and John Edwards will be sworn in as vice president, and this country will reclaim its promise, and out of this long political darkness a brighter day will come. Thank you very much everybody. God bless you.

2 "The audacity to hope."

A More Perfect Union
18 March 2008
National Constitution Center, Philadelphia,
Pennsylvania

Responding to a spike in the attention paid to controversial remarks made by Jeremiah Wright, his former pastor and, until shortly before the speech, a participant in his campaign. Obama frames his response in terms of the broader issue of race in the United States. The title of the speech is taken from the Preamble to the United States Constitution.

"We the people, in order to form a more perfect union." Two hundred and twenty one years ago, in a hall that still stands across the street, a group of men gathered and, with these simple words, launched America's improbable experiment in democracy. Farmers and scholars, statesmen and patriots who had traveled across the ocean to escape tyranny and persecution finally made real their Declaration of Independence at a Philadelphia convention that lasted through the spring of 1787.

The document they produced was eventually signed, but ultimately unfinished. It was stained by this nation's original sin of slavery, a question that divided the colonies and brought the convention to a stalemate until the founders chose to allow the slave trade to continue for at least 20 more years, and to leave any final resolution to future generations.

Of course, the answer to the slavery question was already embedded within our Constitution - a Constitution that had at is very core the ideal of equal citizenship under the law; a Constitution that promised its people liberty and justice; and a union that could be and should be perfected over time.

And yet words on a parchment would not be enough to deliver slaves from bondage, or provide men and women of every color and creed their full rights and obligations as citizens of the United States. What would be needed were Americans in successive generations who were willing to do their part - through protests and struggles, on the streets and in the courts, through a civil war and civil disobedience, and always at great risk - to narrow that gap between the promise of our ideals and the reality of their time.

This was one of the tasks we set forth at the beginning of this presidential campaign. To continue the long march of those who came before us. A march for a more just, more equal, more free, more caring, and more prosperous America.

I chose to run for President at this moment in history

because I believe deeply that we cannot solve the challenges of our time unless we solve them together. Unless we perfect our union by understanding that we may have different stories, but we hold common hopes.

That we may not look the same and may not have come from the same place, but we all want to move in the same direction: towards a better future for our children and our grandchildren. And this belief comes from my unyielding faith in the decency and generosity of the American people.   But it also comes from my own story.

I'm the son of a black man from Kenya and a white woman from Kansas. I was raised with the help of a white grandfather who survived a Depression to serve in Patton's army during World War II, and a white grandmother who worked on a bomber assembly line at Fort Leavenworth while he was overseas. I've gone to some of the best schools in America and I've lived in one of the world's poorest nations.

I am married to a black American who carries within her the blood of slaves and slave owners, an inheritance we pass on to our two precious daughters. I have brothers, sisters, nieces, nephews, uncles, and cousins of every race and every hue scattered across three continents. And for as long as I live, I will never forget that in no other country on earth is my story even possible. It's a story that hasn't made me the most conventional of candidates. But it is a story that has seared into my genetic makeup the idea that this nation is more than the sum of its parts – that out of many, we are truly one.

Now throughout the first year of this campaign, against all predictions to the contrary, we saw how hungry the American people were for this message of unity. Despite the temptation to view my candidacy through a purely racial lens, we won commanding victories in states with some of the whitest populations in the country. In South Carolina, where the Confederate flag still flies, we built a powerful coalition of African Americans and white Americans.

This is not to say that race has not been an issue in this campaign. At various stages in the campaign, some commentators have deemed me either "too black" or "not black enough." We saw racial tensions bubble to the surface during the week before the South Carolina primary. The press has scoured every single exit poll for the latest evidence of racial polarization, not just in terms of white and black, but black and brown as well.

And yet, it's only been in the last couple of weeks that the discussion of race in this campaign has taken a particularly divisive turn. On one end of the spectrum, we've heard the implication that my candidacy is somehow an exercise in affirmative action; that it's based solely on the desire of wild and wide-eyed liberals to purchase racial reconciliation on the cheap.

On the other end, we've heard my former pastor, Jeremiah Wright, use incendiary language to express views that have the potential not only to widen the racial divide, but views that denigrate both the greatness and the goodness of our nation and that rightly offend white and black alike.

Now I've already condemned, in unequivocal terms, the statements of Reverend Wright that have caused such controversy, and in some cases, pain. For some, nagging questions remain: Did I know him to be an occasionally fierce critic of American domestic and foreign policy? Of course. Did I ever hear him make remarks that could be considered controversial while I sat in the church? Yes. Did I strongly disagree with many of his political views? Absolutely, just as I'm sure many of you have heard remarks from your pastors, priests, or rabbis with which you strongly disagree.

But the remarks that have caused this recent firestorm weren't simply controversial. They weren't simply a religious leader's efforts to speak out against perceived injustice. Instead, they expressed a profoundly distorted view of this country, a view that sees white racism as endemic and that elevates what is wrong with America above all that we know is right with America; a view that sees the conflicts in the Middle East as rooted primarily in the actions of stalwart allies like Israel instead of emanating from the perverse and hateful ideologies of radical Islam.

As such, Reverend Wright's comments were not only wrong but divisive, divisive at a time when we need unity; racially charged at a time when we need to come together to solve a set of monumental problems: two wars, a terrorist threat, a falling economy, a chronic health care crisis, and potentially devastating climate change. Problems that are neither black or white or Latino or Asian, but rather problems that confront us all.

Given my background, my politics, and my professed values and ideals, there will no doubt be those for whom my statements of condemnation are not enough. Why associate myself with Reverend Wright in the first place, they may ask? Why not join another church? And I confess that if all that I knew of Reverend Wright were the snippets of those sermons that have run in an endless loop on the television sets and YouTube, if Trinity United Church of Christ conformed to the caricatures being peddled by some commentators, there is no doubt that I would react in much the same way.

But the truth is, that isn't all that I know of the man. The man I met more than twenty years ago is a man who helped introduce me to my Christian faith, a man who spoke to me about our obligations to love one another, to care for the sick and lift up the poor. He is a man who served his country as a United States Marine, and who has studied and lectured at some of the finest universities and seminaries in the country, and who over 30 years has led a church that serves the community by doing God's work here on Earth – by housing the homeless, ministering to the needy, providing day care services and scholarships and prison ministries, and reaching out to those suffering from HIV/AIDS.

In my first book, Dreams From My Father, I described the experience of my first service at Trinity, and it goes as follows:
People began to shout, to rise from their seats and clap and cry out, a forceful wind carrying the

reverend's voice up to the rafters.

And in that single note - hope - I heard something else; at the foot of that cross, inside the thousands of churches across the city, I imagined the stories of ordinary black people merging with the stories of David and Goliath, Moses and Pharaoh, the Christians in the lion's den, Ezekiel's field of dry bones.

Those stories of survival and freedom and hope became our stories, my story. The blood that spilled was our blood; the tears our tears; until this black church, on this bright day, seemed once more a vessel carrying the story of a people into future generations and into a larger world. Our trials and triumphs became at once unique and universal, black and more than black. In chronicling our journey, the stories and songs gave us a meaning to reclaim memories that we didn't need to feel shame about. Memories that all people might study and cherish and with which we could start to rebuild.

That has been my experience at Trinity. Like other predominantly black churches across the country, Trinity embodies the black community in its entirety - the doctor and the welfare mom, the model student and the former gang-banger. Like other black churches, Trinity's services are full of raucous laughter and sometimes bawdy humor. They are full of dancing and clapping and screaming and shouting that may seem jarring to the untrained ear. The church contains in full the kindness and cruelty, the fierce intelligence and the shocking ignorance, the struggles and successes, the love and, yes, the bitterness and biases that make up the black experience in America.

And this helps explain, perhaps, my relationship with Reverend Wright. As imperfect as he may be, he has been like family to me. He strengthens my faith, officiated my wedding, and baptized my children . Not once in my conversations with him have I heard him talk about any ethnic group in derogatory terms or treat whites with whom he interacted with anything but courtesy and respect. He contains within him the contradictions – the good and the bad – of the community that he has served diligently for so many years.

I can no more disown him than I can disown the black community. I can no more disown him than I can disown my white grandmother, a woman who helped raise me, a woman who sacrificed again and again for me, a woman who loves me as much as she loves anything in this world, but a woman who once confessed her fear of black men who passed her by on the street, and who on more than one occasion has uttered racial or ethnic stereotypes that made me cringe.

These people are part of me. And they are part of America, this country that I love.

Now, some will see this as an attempt to justify or excuse comments that are simply inexcusable. I can assure you it is not. And I suppose the politically safe thing to do would be to move on from this episode and just hope that it fades into the woodwork. We can dismiss Reverend Wright as a crank or a demagogue, just as some have dismissed Geraldine

Ferraro in the aftermath of her recent statements as harboring some deep - deep-seated bias.

But race is an issue that I believe this nation cannot afford to ignore right now. We would be making the same mistake that Reverend Wright made in his offending sermons about America: to simplify and stereotype and amplify the negative to the point that it distorts reality.

The fact is that the comments that have been made and the issues that have surfaced over the last few weeks reflect the complexities of race in this country that we've never really worked through, a part of our union that we have not yet made perfect. And if we walk away now, if we simply retreat into our respective corners, we will never be able to come together and solve challenges like health care or education or the need to find good jobs for every American.

Understanding -- Understanding this reality requires a reminder of how we arrived at this point. As William Faulkner once wrote, "The past isn't dead and buried. In fact, it isn't even past." We do not need to recite here the history of racial injustice in this country.

But we do need to remind ourselves that so many of the disparities that exist between the African-American community and the larger American community today can be traced directly to inequalities passed on from an earlier generation that suffered under the brutal legacy of slavery and Jim Crow. Segregated schools were, and are, inferior schools. We still haven't fixed them, 50 years after Brown versus Board of Education. And the inferior education they provided, then and now, helps explain the pervasive achievement gap between today's black and white students.

Legalized discrimination, where blacks were prevented, often through violence, from owning property, or loans were not granted to African-American business owners, or black homeowners could not access FHA mortgages, or blacks were excluded from unions, or the police force, or the fire department meant that black families could not amass any meaningful wealth to bequeath to future generations.

That history helps explain the wealth and income gap between blacks and whites and the concentrated pockets of poverty that persist in so many of today's urban and rural communities. A lack of economic opportunity among black men and the shame and frustration that came from not being able to provide for one's family contributed to the erosion of black families, a problem that welfare policies for many years may have worsened.

And the lack of basic services in so many urban black neighborhoods - parks for kids to play in, police walking the beat, regular garbage pick-up, building code enforcement - all helped create a cycle of violence, blight, and neglect that continues to haunt us.

This is the reality in which Reverend Wright and other African-Americans of his generation grew up.

They came of age in the late '50s and early '60s, a time when segregation was still the law of the land and opportunity was systematically constricted.

What's remarkable is not how many failed in the face of discrimination, but how many men and women overcame the odds, how many were able to make a way out of no way for those like me who would come after them.

But for all those who scratched and clawed their way to get a piece of the American Dream, there were many who didn't make it. Those who were ultimately defeated, in one way or another, by discrimination. That legacy of defeat was passed on to future generations - those young men and increasingly young women who we see standing on street corners or languishing in our prisons, without hope or prospects for the future.

Even for those blacks who did make it, questions of race, and racism, continue to define their world view in fundamental ways. For the men and women of Reverend Wright's generation, the memories of humiliation and doubt and fear have not gone away, nor has the anger and the bitterness of those years.

That anger may not get expressed in public, in front of white co-workers or white friends, but it does find voice in the barbershop or the beauty shop or around the kitchen table. At times, that anger is exploited by politicians to gin up votes along racial lines or to make up for a politician's own failings. And occasionally it finds voice in the church on Sunday morning, in the pulpit and in the pews.

The fact that so many people are surprised to hear that anger in some of Reverend Wright's sermons simply reminds us of that old truism that the most segregated hour of American life occurs on Sunday morning.

That -- That anger is not always productive. Indeed, all too often it distracts attention from solving real problems. It keeps us from squarely facing our own complicity within the African-American community in our own condition. It prevents the African-American community from forging the alliances it needs to bring about real change. But the anger is real; it is powerful, and to simply wish it away, to condemn it without understanding its roots only serves to widen the chasm of misunderstanding that exists between the races.

In fact, a similar anger exists within segments of the white community. Most working and middle-class white Americans don't feel that they've been particularly privileged by their race. Their experience is the immigrant experience. As far as they're concerned, no one handed them anything; they built it from scratch. They've worked hard all their lives, many times only to see their jobs shipped overseas or their pensions dumped after a lifetime of labor.

They are anxious about their futures, and they feel their dreams slipping away. And in an era of stagnant wages and global competition, opportunity comes to be seen as a zero sum game, in which your dreams come at my expense. So when they are told to bus their children to a school across town, when they hear that an African American is getting an advantage in landing a good job or a spot in a good college because of an injustice that they themselves never committed, when they're told that their fears about crime in urban neighborhoods are somehow prejudice, resentment builds over time.

Like the anger within the black community, these resentments aren't always expressed in polite company. But they have helped shape the political landscape for at least a generation. Anger over welfare and affirmative action helped forge the Reagan Coalition. Politicians routinely exploited fears of crime for their own electoral ends. Talk show hosts and conservative commentators built entire careers unmasking bogus claims of racism while dismissing legitimate discussions of racial injustice and inequality as mere political correctness or reverse racism.

And just as black anger often proved counterproductive, so have these white resentments distracted attention from the real culprits of the middle class squeeze: a corporate culture rife with inside dealing, questionable accounting practices, and short-term greed; a Washington dominated by lobbyists and special interests; economic policies that favor the few over the many. And yet, to wish away the resentments of white Americans, to label them as misguided or even racist without recognizing they are grounded in legitimate concerns, this, too, widens the racial divide and blocks the path to understanding.

This is where we are right now.

It's a racial stalemate we've been stuck in for years. And contrary to the claims of some of my critics, black and white, I have never been so naive as to believe that we can get beyond our racial divisions in a single election cycle or with a single candidate, particularly -- particularly a candidacy as imperfect as my own.

But I have asserted a firm conviction, a conviction rooted in my faith in God and my faith in the American people, that, working together, we can move beyond some of our old racial wounds and that, in fact, we have no choice. We have no choice if we are to continue on the path of a more perfect union.

For the African-American community, that path means embracing the burdens of our past without becoming victims of our past. It means continuing to insist on a full measure of justice in every aspect of American life. But it also means binding our particular grievances, for better health care and better schools and better jobs, to the larger aspirations of all Americans - the white woman struggling to break the glass ceiling, the white man who's been laid off, the immigrant trying to feed his family.

And it means also taking full responsibility for our own lives - by demanding more from our fathers, and spending more time with our children, and reading to them, and teaching them that while they may face challenges and discrimination in their own lives, they must never succumb to despair or cynicism. They must always believe -- They must always believe that they can write their own destiny.

Ironically, this quintessentially American - and, yes, conservative - notion of self-help found frequent expression in Reverend Wright's sermons. But what my former pastor too often failed to understand is that embarking on a program of self-help also requires a belief that society can change. The profound mistake of Reverend Wright's sermons is not that he spoke about racism in our society. It's that he spoke as if our society was static, as if no progress had been made, as if this country - a country that has made it possible for one of his own members to run for the highest office in the land and build a coalition of white and black, Latino, Asian, rich, poor, young and old - is still irrevocably bound to a tragic past.

What we know, what we have seen, is that America can change. That is true genius of this nation. What we have already achieved gives us hope - the audacity to hope - for what we can and must achieve tomorrow.

Now, in the white community, the path to a more perfect union means acknowledging that what ails the African-American community does not just exist in the minds of black people; that the legacy of discrimination - and current incidents of discrimination, while less overt than in the past - that these things are real and must be addressed.

Not just with words, but with deeds - by investing in our schools and our communities; by enforcing our civil rights laws and ensuring fairness in our criminal justice system; by providing this generation with ladders of opportunity that were unavailable for previous generations. It requires all Americans to realize that your dreams do not have to come at the expense of my dreams, that investing in the health, welfare, and education of black and brown and white children will ultimately help all of America prosper.

In the end, then, what is called for is nothing more and nothing less than what all the world's great religions demand: that we do unto others as we would have them do unto us. Let us be our brother's keeper, Scripture tells us. Let us be our sister's keeper. Let us find that common stake we all have in one another, and let our politics reflect that spirit as well.

For we have a choice in this country.

We can accept a politics that breeds division and conflict and cynicism. We can tackle race only as spectacle, as we did in the O.J. trial; or in the wake of tragedy, as we did in the aftermath of Katrina; or as fodder for the nightly news. We can play Reverend Wright's sermons on every channel every day and talk about them from now until the election, and make the only question in this campaign whether or not the American people think that I somehow believe or sympathize with his most offensive words. We can pounce on some gaffe by a Hillary supporter as evidence that she's playing the race card; or we can speculate on whether white men will all flock to John McCain in the general election regardless of his policies.

We can do that. But if we do, I can tell you that in the next election, we'll be talking about some other distraction, and then another one, and then another one. And nothing will change.

That is one option.

Or, at this moment, in this election, we can come together and say, "Not this time." This time we want to talk about the crumbling schools that are stealing the future of black children and white children and Asian children and Hispanic children and Native-American children. This time we want to reject the cynicism that tells us that these kids can't learn; that those kids who don't look like us are somebody else's problem. The children of America are not "those kids," they are our kids, and we will not let them fall behind in a 21st-century economy.

Not this time . This time we want to talk about how the lines in the emergency room are filled with whites and blacks and Hispanics who do not have health care, who don't have the power on their own to overcome the special interests in Washington, but who can take them on if we do it together.

This time we want to talk about the shuttered mills that once provided a decent life for men and women of every race, and the homes for sale that once belonged to Americans from every religion, every region, every walk of life. This time we want to talk about the fact that the real problem is not that someone who doesn't look like you might take your job; it's that the corporation you work for will ship it overseas for nothing more than a profit.

This time -- This time we want to talk about the men and women of every color and creed who serve together, and fight together, and bleed together under the same proud flag. We want to talk about how to bring them home from a war that should've never been authorized and should've never been waged. And we want to talk about how we'll show our patriotism by caring for them, and their families, and giving them the benefits that they have earned.

I would not be running for President if I didn't believe with all my heart that this is what the vast majority of Americans want for this country. This union may never be perfect, but generation after generation has shown that it can always be perfected. And today, whenever I find myself feeling doubtful or cynical about this possibility, what gives me the most hope is the next generation - the young people whose attitudes and beliefs and openness to change have already made history in this election.

There's one story in particular that I'd like to leave you with today, a story I told when I had the great honor of speaking on Dr. King's birthday at his home church, Ebenezer Baptist, in Atlanta. There's a young, 23-year-old woman, a white woman named Ashley Baia, who organized for our campaign in Florence, South Carolina.

She'd been working to organize a mostly African-American community since the beginning of this campaign, and one day she was at a roundtable discussion where everyone went around telling their story and why they were there. And Ashley said that when she was 9 years old, her mother got cancer. And because she had to miss days of work, she was let go and lost her health care. They had to file for bankruptcy, and that's when Ashley decided that she had to do something to help her mom.

She knew that food was one of their most expensive costs, and so Ashley convinced her mother that what she really liked and really wanted to eat more than anything else was mustard and relish sandwiches - because that was the cheapest way to eat. That's the mind of a 9 year old. She did this for a year until her mom got better. And so Ashley told everyone at the roundtable that the reason she had joined our campaign was so that she could help the millions of other children in the country who want and need to help their parents too.

Now, Ashley might have made a different choice. Perhaps somebody told her along the way that the source of her mother's problems were blacks who were on welfare and too lazy to work, or Hispanics who were coming into the country illegally. But she didn't. She sought out allies in her fight against injustice.

Anyway, Ashley finishes her story and then goes around the room and asks everyone else why they're supporting the campaign. They all have different stories and different reasons. Many bring up a specific issue. And finally they come to this elderly black man who's been sitting there quietly the entire time. And Ashley asks him why he's there. And he doesn't bring up a specific issue. He does not say health care or the economy. He does not say education or the war. He does not say that he was there because of Barack Obama. He simply says to everyone in the room, "I am here because of Ashley." "I'm here because of Ashley."

Now, by itself, that single moment of recognition between that young white girl and that old black man is not enough. It is not enough to give health care to the sick, or jobs to the jobless, or education to our children. But it is where we start. It is where our union grows stronger. And as so many generations have come to realize over the course of the 221 years since a band of patriots signed that document right here in Philadelphia, that is where perfection begins.

Thank you very much, everyone. Thank you.

3 "Change has come to America."

Election Victory Speech
November 4, 2008
Grant Park, Chicago, Illinois

Victory speech at Grant Park in his home city of Chicago, Illinois, before an estimated crowd of 240,000. Viewed by millions around the globe, Obama's speech focuses on the major issues facing the United States and the world, all echoed through his campaign slogan of change. He also mentions his maternal grandmother Madelyn Dunham, who had died just two nights earlier.

Hello Chicago!

If there is anyone out there who still doubts that America is a place where all things are possible; who still wonders if the dream of our founders is alive in our time; who still questions the power of our democracy, tonight is your answer.

It's the answer told by lines that stretched around schools and churches in numbers this nation has never seen; by people who waited three hours and four hours, many for the very first time in their lives, because they believed that this time must be different; that their voices could be that difference.

It's the answer spoken by young and old, rich and poor, Democrat and Republican, black, white, Hispanic, Asian, Native American, gay, straight, disabled and not disabled, Americans who sent a message to the world that we have never been just a collection of individuals or a collection of red states and blue states. We are, and always will be, the United States of America.

It's the answer that led those who've been told for so long, by so many to be cynical and fearful and doubtful about what we can achieve, to put their hands on the arc of history and bend it once more toward the hope of a better day. It's been a long time coming, but tonight, because of what we did on this day, in this election, at this defining moment, change has come to America.

A little bit earlier this evening, I received an extraordinarily gracious call from Senator McCain. Senator McCain fought long and hard in this campaign. And he's fought even longer and harder for the country that he loves. He has endured sacrifices for America that most of us cannot begin to imagine. We are better off for the service rendered by this brave and selfless leader. I congratulate him; I congratulate Governor (Sarah) Palin for all that they've achieved. And I look forward to working with them to renew this nation's promise in the months ahead.

I want to thank my partner in this journey, a man who campaigned from his heart, and spoke for the men and women he grew up with on the streets of Scranton, and rode with on the train home to Delaware, the vice president-elect of the United States, Joe Biden.

And I would not be standing here tonight without the unyielding support of my best friend for the last 16 years, the rock of our family, the love of my life, the nation's next first lady Michelle Obama. Sasha and Malia I love you both more than you can imagine. And you have earned the new puppy that's coming with us to the new White House.

And while she's no longer with us, I know my grandmother's watching, along with the family that made me who I am. I miss them tonight. I know that my debt to them is beyond measure. To my sister Maya, my sister Alma, all my other brothers and sisters, thank you so much for all the support that you've given me. I am grateful to them.

And to my campaign manager, David Plouffe, the unsung hero of this campaign, who built the best - the best political campaign, I think, in the history of the United States of America. To my chief strategist David Axelrod who's been a partner with me every step of the way. To the best campaign team ever assembled in the history of politics, you made this happen and I am forever grateful for what you've sacrificed to get it done.

But above all, I will never forget who this victory truly belongs to. It belongs to you. It belongs to you.

I was never the likeliest candidate for this office. We didn't start with much money or many endorsements. Our campaign was not hatched in the halls of Washington. It began in the backyards of Des Moines and the living rooms of Concord and the front porches of Charleston.

It was built by working men and women who dug into what little savings they had to give 5 dollars and 10 dollars and 20 dollars to the cause. It grew strength from the young people who rejected the myth of their generation's apathy, who left their homes and their families for jobs that offered little pay and less sleep.

It drew strength from the not-so-young people who braved the bitter cold and scorching heat to knock on doors of perfect strangers, and from the millions of Americans who volunteered and organised and proved that more than two centuries later a government of the people, by the people, and for the people has not perished from the Earth.
This is your victory.

And I know you didn't do this just to win an election. And I know you didn't do it for me. You did it because you understand the enormity of the task that lies ahead. For even as we celebrate tonight, we know the challenges that tomorrow will bring are the greatest of our lifetime - two wars, a planet in peril, the worst financial crisis in a century.

Even as we stand here tonight, we know there are brave Americans waking up in the deserts of Iraq and the mountains of Afghanistan to risk their lives for us.

There are mothers and fathers who will lie awake after the children fall asleep and wonder how they'll make the mortgage or pay their doctors' bills or save enough for their child's college education.

There's new energy to harness, new jobs to be created, new schools to build, and threats to meet, alliances to repair.

The road ahead will be long. Our climb will be steep. We may not get there in one year or even in one term. But, America, I have never been more hopeful than I am tonight that we will get there. I promise you, we as a people will get there. There will be setbacks and false starts. There are many who won't agree with every decision or policy I make as president. And we know the government can't solve every problem.

But I will always be honest with you about the challenges we face. I will listen to you, especially when we disagree. And, above all, I will ask you to join in the work of remaking this nation, the only way it's been done in America for 221 years - block by block, brick by brick, calloused hand by calloused hand. What began 21 months ago in the depths of winter cannot end on this autumn night.

This victory alone is not the change we seek. It is only the chance for us to make that change. And that cannot happen if we go back to the way things were. It can't happen without you, without a new spirit of service, a new spirit of sacrifice.

So let us summon a new spirit of patriotism, of responsibility, where each of us resolves to pitch in and work harder and look after not only ourselves but each other. Let us remember that, if this financial crisis taught us anything, it's that we cannot have a thriving Wall Street while Main Street suffers.

In this country, we rise or fall as one nation, as one people. Let's resist the temptation to fall back on the same partisanship and pettiness and immaturity that has poisoned our politics for so long. Let's remember that it was a man from this state who first carried the banner of the Republican Party to the White House, a party founded on the values of self-reliance and individual liberty and national unity. Those are values that we all share. And while the Democratic Party has won a great victory tonight, we do so with a measure of humility and determination to heal the divides that have held back our progress.

As Lincoln said to a nation far more divided than ours, we are not enemies but friends. Though passion may have strained, it must not break our bonds of affection. And to those Americans whose support I have yet to earn, I may not have won your vote tonight, but I hear your voices. I need your help. And I will be your president, too.

And to all those watching tonight from beyond our shores, from parliaments and palaces, to those who are huddled around radios in the forgotten corners of the world, our stories are singular, but our destiny is shared, and a new dawn of American leadership is at hand.

To those – to those who would tear the world down: We will defeat you. To those who seek peace and security: We support you. And to all those who have wondered if America's beacon still burns as bright: Tonight we proved once more that the true strength of our nation comes not from the might of our arms or the scale of our wealth, but from the enduring power of our ideals: democracy, liberty, opportunity and unyielding hope.

That's the true genius of America: that America can change. Our union can be perfected. What we've already achieved gives us hope for what we can and must achieve tomorrow.

This election had many firsts and many stories that will be told for generations. But one that's on my mind tonight's about a woman who cast her ballot in Atlanta. She's a lot like the millions of others who stood in line to make their voice heard in this election except for one thing: Ann Nixon Cooper is 106 years old.

She was born just a generation past slavery; a time when there were no cars on the road or planes in the sky; when someone like her couldn't vote for two reasons – because she was a woman and because of the colour of her skin.

And tonight, I think about all that she's seen throughout her century in America – the heartache and the hope; the struggle and the progress; the times we were told that we can't, and the people who pressed on with that American creed: Yes we can.

At a time when women's voices were silenced and their hopes dismissed, she lived to see them stand up and speak out and reach for the ballot. Yes we can.

When there was despair in the dust bowl and depression across the land, she saw a nation conquer fear itself with a New Deal, new jobs, a new sense of common purpose. Yes we can.

When the bombs fell on our harbour and tyranny threatened the world, she was there to witness a generation rise to greatness and a democracy was saved. Yes we can.

She was there for the buses in Montgomery, the hoses in Birmingham, a bridge in Selma, and a preacher from Atlanta who told a people that 'We Shall Overcome'. Yes we can.

A man touched down on the moon, a wall came down in Berlin, a world was connected by our own science and imagination.

And this year, in this election, she touched her finger to a screen, and cast her vote, because after 106 years in America, through the best of times and the darkest of hours, she knows how America can change. Yes we can.

America, we have come so far. We have seen so much. But there is so much more to do. So tonight, let us ask ourselves - if our children should live to see the next century; if my daughters should be so lucky to live as long as Ann Nixon Cooper, what change will they see? What progress will we have made?

This is our chance to answer that call. This is our moment.

This is our time, to put our people back to work and open doors of opportunity for our kids; to restore prosperity and promote the cause of peace; to reclaim the American dream and reaffirm that fundamental truth, that, out of many, we are one; that while we breathe, we hope. And where we are met with cynicism and doubts and those who tell us that we can't, we will respond with that timeless creed that sums up the spirit of a people: Yes, we can.

"Thank you. God bless you. And may God bless the United States of America."

I spent a few months researching articles on the best speeches in the eyes of President Barack Obama's White House staffers, speechwriters, and those who witnessed them.

4 "The character of our country."

Address to Joint Session of Congress on Health Insurance Reform
September 9, 2009
U.S. Capitol, Washington, D.C.

Madam Speaker, Vice President Biden, members of Congress, and the American people:
When I spoke here last winter, this nation was facing the worst economic crisis since the Great Depression. We were losing an average of 700,000 jobs per month. Credit was frozen. And our financial system was on the verge of collapse.

As any American who is still looking for work or a way to pay their bills will tell you, we are by no means out of the woods. A full and vibrant recovery is still many months away. And I will not let up until those Americans who seek jobs can find them; until those businesses that seek capital and credit can thrive; until all responsible homeowners can stay in their homes.

That is our ultimate goal. But thanks to the bold and

decisive action we've taken since January, I can stand here with confidence and say that we have pulled this economy back from the brink.

I want to thank the members of this body for your efforts and your support in these last several months, and especially those who've taken the difficult votes that have put us on a path to recovery. I also want to thank the American people for their patience and resolve during this trying time for our nation.

But we did not come here just to clean up crises. We came here to build a future. So tonight, I return to speak to all of you about an issue that is central to that future -- and that is the issue of health care.

I am not the first President to take up this cause, but I am determined to be the last. It has now been nearly a century since Theodore Roosevelt first called for health care reform. And ever since, nearly every President and Congress, whether Democrat or Republican, has attempted to meet this challenge in some way. A bill for comprehensive health reform was first introduced by John Dingell Sr. in 1943. Sixty-five years later, his son continues to introduce that same bill at the beginning of each session.

Our collective failure to meet this challenge -- year after year, decade after decade -- has led us to the breaking point. Everyone understands the extraordinary hardships that are placed on the uninsured, who live every day just one accident or illness away from bankruptcy. These are not primarily people on welfare. These are middle-class Americans. Some can't get insurance on the job.

Others are self-employed, and can't afford it, since buying insurance on your own costs you three times as much as the coverage you get from your employer. Many other Americans who are willing and able to pay are still denied insurance due to previous illnesses or conditions that insurance companies decide are too risky or too expensive to cover.

We are the only democracy -- the only advanced democracy on Earth -- the only wealthy nation -- that allows such hardship for millions of its people. There are now more than 30 million American citizens who cannot get coverage. In just a two-year period, one in every three Americans goes without health care coverage at some point. And every day, 14,000 Americans lose their coverage. In other words, it can happen to anyone.

But the problem that plagues the health care system is not just a problem for the uninsured.

Those who do have insurance have never had less security and stability than they do today. More and more Americans worry that if you move, lose your job, or change your job, you'll lose your health insurance too. More and more Americans pay their premiums, only to discover that their insurance company has dropped their coverage when they get sick, or won't pay the full cost of care. It happens every day.

One man from Illinois lost his coverage in the middle of chemotherapy because his insurer found that he hadn't reported gallstones that he didn't even know about. They delayed his treatment, and he died because of it. Another woman from Texas was about to get a double mastectomy when her insurance company canceled her policy because she forgot to declare a case of acne. By the time she had her insurance reinstated, her breast cancer had more than doubled in size. That is heart-breaking, it is wrong, and no one should be treated that way in the United States of America.

Then there's the problem of rising cost. We spend one and a half times more per person on health care than any other country, but we aren't any healthier for it. This is one of the reasons that insurance premiums have gone up three times faster than wages. It's why so many employers -- especially small businesses -- are forcing their employees to pay more for insurance, or are dropping their coverage entirely. It's why so many aspiring entrepreneurs cannot afford to open a business in the first place, and why American businesses that compete internationally -- like our automakers -- are at a huge disadvantage. And it's why those of us with health insurance are also paying a hidden and growing tax for those without it -- about $1,000 per year that pays for somebody else's emergency room and charitable care.

Finally, our health care system is placing an unsustainable burden on taxpayers. When health care costs grow at the rate they have, it puts greater pressure on programs like Medicare and Medicaid. If we do nothing to slow these skyrocketing costs, we will eventually be spending more on Medicare and Medicaid than every other government program combined. Put simply, our health care problem is our deficit problem. Nothing else even comes close. Nothing else.

Now, these are the facts. Nobody disputes them. We know we must reform this system. The question is how.

There are those on the left who believe that the only way to fix the system is through a single-payer system like Canada's -- where we would severely restrict the private insurance market and have the government provide coverage for everybody. On the right, there are those who argue that we should end employer-based systems and leave individuals to buy health insurance on their own.

I've said -- I have to say that there are arguments to be made for both these approaches. But either one would represent a radical shift that would disrupt the health care most people currently have. Since health care represents one-sixth of our economy, I believe it makes more sense to build on what works and fix what doesn't, rather than try to build an entirely new system from scratch. And that is precisely what those of you in Congress have tried to do over the past several months.

During that time, we've seen Washington at its best and at its worst.

We've seen many in this chamber work tirelessly for the better part of this year to offer thoughtful ideas about how to achieve reform. Of the five committees asked to develop bills, four have completed their work, and the Senate Finance Committee announced today that it will move forward next week. That has never happened before. Our overall efforts have been supported by an unprecedented coalition of doctors and nurses; hospitals, seniors' groups, and even drug companies -- many of whom opposed reform in the past. And there is agreement in this chamber on about 80 percent of what needs to be done, putting us closer to the goal of reform than we have ever been.

But what we've also seen in these last months is the same partisan spectacle that only hardens the disdain many Americans have towards their own government. Instead of honest debate, we've seen scare tactics. Some have dug into unyielding ideological camps that offer no hope of compromise. Too many have used this as an opportunity to score short-term political points, even if it robs the country of our opportunity to solve a long-term challenge. And out of this blizzard of charges and counter-charges, confusion has reigned.

Well, the time for bickering is over. The time for games has passed. Now is the season for action. Now is when we must bring the best ideas of both parties together, and show the American people that we can still do what we were sent here to do. Now is the time to deliver on health care. Now is the time to deliver on health care.

The plan I'm announcing tonight would meet three basic goals. It will provide more security and stability to those who have health insurance. It will provide insurance for those who don't. And it will slow the growth of health care costs for our families, our businesses, and our government.

It's a plan that asks everyone to take responsibility for meeting this challenge -- not just government, not just insurance companies, but everybody including employers and individuals. And it's a plan that incorporates ideas from senators and congressmen, from Democrats and Republicans -- and yes, from some of my opponents in both the primary and general election.

Here are the details that every American needs to know about this plan. First, if you are among the hundreds of millions of Americans who already have health insurance through your job, or Medicare, or Medicaid, or the VA, nothing in this plan will require you or your employer to change the coverage or the doctor you have. Let me repeat this: Nothing in our plan requires you to change what you have.

What this plan will do is make the insurance you have work better for you. Under this plan, it will be against the law for insurance companies to deny you coverage because of a preexisting condition.

As soon as I sign this bill, it will be against the law for insurance companies to drop your coverage when you get sick or water it down when you need it the most. They will no longer be able to place some arbitrary cap on the amount of coverage you can receive in a given year or in a lifetime. We will place a limit on how much you can be charged for out-of-pocket expenses, because in the United States of America, no one should go broke because they get sick. And insurance companies will be required to cover, with no extra charge, routine checkups and preventive care, like mammograms and colonoscopies -- because there's no reason we shouldn't be catching diseases like breast cancer and colon cancer before they get worse. That makes sense, it saves money, and it saves lives.

Now, that's what Americans who have health insurance can expect from this plan -- more security and more stability.

Now, if you're one of the tens of millions of Americans who don't currently have health insurance, the second part of this plan will finally offer you quality, affordable choices.

If you lose your job or you change your job, you'll be able to get coverage. If you strike out on your own and start a small business, you'll be able to get coverage. We'll do this by creating a new insurance exchange -- a marketplace where individuals and small businesses will be able to shop for health insurance at competitive prices.

Insurance companies will have an incentive to participate in this exchange because it lets them compete for millions of new customers. As one big group, these customers will have greater leverage to bargain with the insurance companies for better prices and quality coverage. This is how large companies and government employees get affordable insurance. It's how everyone in this Congress gets affordable insurance. And it's time to give every American the same opportunity that we give ourselves.

Now, for those individuals and small businesses who still can't afford the lower-priced insurance available in the exchange, we'll provide tax credits, the size of which will be based on your need. And all insurance companies that want access to this new marketplace will have to abide by the consumer protections I already mentioned.

This exchange will take effect in four years, which will give us time to do it right. In the meantime, for those Americans who can't get insurance today because they have preexisting medical conditions, we will immediately offer low-cost coverage that will protect you against financial ruin if you become seriously ill.

This was a good idea when Senator John McCain proposed it in the campaign, it's a good idea now, and we should all embrace it.

Now, even if we provide these affordable options, there may be those -- especially the young and the healthy -- who still want to take the risk and go without coverage. There may still be companies that refuse to do right by their workers by giving them coverage.

The problem is, such irresponsible behavior costs all the rest of us money. If there are affordable options and people still don't sign up for health insurance, it means we pay for these people's expensive emergency room visits. If some businesses don't provide workers health care, it forces the rest of us to pick up the tab when their workers get sick, and gives those businesses an unfair advantage over their competitors. And unless everybody does their part, many of the insurance reforms we seek -- especially requiring insurance companies to cover preexisting conditions -- just can't be achieved.

And that's why under my plan, individuals will be required to carry basic health insurance -- just as most states require you to carry auto insurance. Likewise -- likewise, businesses will be required to either offer their workers health care, or chip in to help cover the cost of their workers. There will be a hardship waiver for those individuals who still can't afford coverage, and 95 percent of all small businesses, because of their size and narrow profit margin, would be exempt from these requirements.

But we can't have large businesses and individuals who can afford coverage game the system by avoiding responsibility to themselves or their employees. Improving our health care system only works if everybody does their part.

And while there remain some significant details to be ironed out, I believe -- I believe a broad consensus exists for the aspects of the plan I just outlined: consumer protections for those with insurance, an exchange that allows individuals and small businesses to purchase affordable coverage, and a requirement that people who can afford insurance get insurance.

And I have no doubt that these reforms would greatly benefit Americans from all walks of life, as well as the economy as a whole. Still, given all the misinformation that's been spread over the past few months, I realize -- I realize that many Americans have grown nervous about reform. So tonight I want to address some of the key controversies that are still out there.

Some of people's concerns have grown out of bogus claims spread by those whose only agenda is to kill reform at any cost. The best example is the claim made not just by radio and cable talk show hosts, but by prominent politicians, that we plan to set up panels of bureaucrats with the power to kill off senior citizens. Now, such a charge would be laughable if it weren't so cynical and irresponsible. It is a lie, plain and simple.

There are also those who claim that our reform efforts would insure illegal immigrants. This, too, is false. The reforms -- the reforms I'm proposing would not apply to those who are here illegally.

AUDIENCE MEMBER: You lie! (Boos.)

It's not true. And one more misunderstanding I want to clear up -- under our plan, no federal dollars will be used to fund abortions, and federal conscience laws will remain in place.

Now, my health care proposal has also been attacked by some who oppose reform as a "government takeover" of the entire health care system. As proof, critics point to a provision in our plan that allows the uninsured and small businesses to choose a publicly sponsored insurance option, administered by the government just like Medicaid or Medicare.

So let me set the record straight here. My guiding principle is, and always has been, that consumers do better when there is choice and competition. That's how the market works. Unfortunately, in 34 states, 75 percent of the insurance market is controlled by five or fewer companies. In Alabama, almost 90 percent is controlled by just one company. And without competition, the price of insurance goes up and quality goes down. And it makes it easier for insurance companies to treat their customers badly -- by cherry-picking the healthiest individuals and trying to drop the sickest, by overcharging small businesses who have no leverage, and by jacking up rates.

Insurance executives don't do this because they're bad people; they do it because it's profitable. As one former insurance executive testified before Congress, insurance companies are not only encouraged to find reasons to drop the seriously ill, they are rewarded for it. All of this is in service of meeting what this former executive called "Wall Street's relentless profit expectations."

Now, I have no interest in putting insurance companies out of business. They provide a legitimate service, and employ a lot of our friends and neighbors. I just want to hold them accountable. And the insurance reforms that I've already mentioned would do just that.

But an additional step we can take to keep insurance companies honest is by making a not-for-profit public option available in the insurance exchange. Now, let me be clear. Let me be clear. It would only be an option for those who don't have insurance. No one would be forced to choose it, and it would not impact those of you who already have insurance. In fact, based on Congressional Budget Office estimates, we believe that less than 5 percent of Americans would sign up.

Despite all this, the insurance companies and their allies don't like this idea. They argue that these private companies can't fairly compete with the government. And they'd be right if taxpayers were subsidizing this public insurance option. But they won't be. I've insisted that like any private insurance company, the public insurance option would have to be self-sufficient and rely on the premiums it collects. But by avoiding some of the overhead that gets eaten up at private companies by profits and excessive administrative costs and executive salaries, it could provide a good deal for consumers, and would also keep pressure on private insurers to keep their policies affordable and treat their customers better, the same way public colleges and universities provide additional choice and competition to students without in any way inhibiting a vibrant system of private colleges and universities.

Now, it is -- it's worth noting that a strong majority of Americans still favor a public insurance option of the sort I've proposed tonight. But its impact shouldn't be exaggerated -- by the left or the right or the media. It is only one part of my plan, and shouldn't be used as a handy excuse for the usual Washington ideological battles. To my progressive friends, I would remind you that for decades, the driving idea behind reform has been to end insurance company abuses and make coverage available for those without it.

The public option -- the public option is only a means to that end -- and we should remain open to other ideas that accomplish our ultimate goal. And to my Republican friends, I say that rather than making wild claims about a government takeover of health care, we should work together to address any legitimate concerns you may have.

For example -- for example, some have suggested that the public option go into effect only in those markets where insurance companies are not providing affordable policies. Others have proposed a co-op or another non-profit entity to administer the plan. These are all constructive ideas worth exploring. But I will not back down on the basic principle that if Americans can't find affordable coverage, we will provide you with a choice.

And I will make sure that no government bureaucrat or insurance company bureaucrat gets between you and the care that you need.

Finally, let me discuss an issue that is a great concern to me, to members of this chamber, and to the public -- and that's how we pay for this plan.

And here's what you need to know. First, I will not sign a plan that adds one dime to our deficits -- either now or in the future. I will not sign it if it adds one dime to the deficit, now or in the future, period. And to prove that I'm serious, there will be a provision in this plan that requires us to come forward with more spending cuts if the savings we promised don't materialize. Now, part of the reason I faced a trillion-dollar deficit when I walked in the door of the White House is because too many initiatives over the last decade were not paid for -- from the Iraq war to tax breaks for the wealthy. I will not make that same mistake with health care.

Second, we've estimated that most of this plan can be paid for by finding savings within the existing health care system, a system that is currently full of waste and abuse. Right now, too much of the hard-earned savings and tax dollars we spend on health care don't make us any healthier. That's not my judgment -- it's the judgment of medical professionals across this country. And this is also true when it comes to Medicare and Medicaid.

In fact, I want to speak directly to seniors for a moment, because Medicare is another issue that's been subjected to demagoguery and distortion during the course of this debate.

More than four decades ago, this nation stood up for the principle that after a lifetime of hard work, our seniors should not be left to struggle with a pile of medical bills in their later years. That's how Medicare was born. And it remains a sacred trust that must be passed down from one generation to the next. And that is why not a dollar of the Medicare trust fund will be used to pay for this plan.

The only thing this plan would eliminate is the hundreds of billions of dollars in waste and fraud, as well as unwarranted subsidies in Medicare that go to insurance companies -- subsidies that do everything to pad their profits but don't improve the care of seniors. And we will also create an independent commission of doctors and medical experts charged with identifying more waste in the years ahead.

Now, these steps will ensure that you -- America's seniors -- get the benefits you've been promised. They will ensure that Medicare is there for future generations. And we can use some of the savings to fill the gap in coverage that forces too many seniors to pay thousands of dollars a year out of their own pockets for prescription drugs.

That's what this plan will do for you. So don't pay attention to those scary stories about how your benefits will be cut, especially since some of the same folks who are spreading these tall tales have fought against Medicare in the past and just this year supported a budget that would essentially have turned Medicare into a privatized voucher program. That will not happen on my watch. I will protect Medicare.

Now, because Medicare is such a big part of the health care system, making the program more efficient can help usher in changes in the way we deliver health care that can reduce costs for everybody. We have long known that some places -- like the Intermountain Healthcare in Utah or the Geisinger Health System in rural Pennsylvania -- offer high-quality care at costs below average. So the commission can help encourage the adoption of these common-sense best practices by doctors and medical professionals throughout the system -- everything from reducing hospital infection rates to encouraging better coordination between teams of doctors.

Reducing the waste and inefficiency in Medicare and Medicaid will pay for most of this plan. Now, much of the rest would be paid for with revenues from the very same drug and insurance companies that stand to benefit from tens of millions of new customers. And this reform will charge insurance companies a fee for their most expensive policies, which will encourage them to provide greater value for the money -- an idea which has the support of Democratic and Republican experts. And according to these same experts, this modest change could help hold down the cost of health care for all of us in the long run.

Now, finally, many in this chamber -- particularly on the Republican side of the aisle -- have long insisted that reforming our medical malpractice laws can help bring down the cost of health care. Now -- there you go. There you go. Now, I don't believe malpractice reform is a silver bullet, but I've talked to enough doctors to know that defensive medicine may be contributing to unnecessary costs. So I'm proposing that we move forward on a range of ideas about how to put patient safety first and let doctors focus on practicing medicine. I know that the Bush administration considered authorizing demonstration projects in individual states to test these ideas. I think it's a good idea, and I'm directing my Secretary of Health and Human Services to move forward on this initiative today.

Now, add it all up, and the plan I'm proposing will

cost around $900 billion over 10 years -- less than we have spent on the Iraq and Afghanistan wars, and less than the tax cuts for the wealthiest few Americans that Congress passed at the beginning of the previous administration. Now, most of these costs will be paid for with money already being spent -- but spent badly -- in the existing health care system. The plan will not add to our deficit. The middle class will realize greater security, not higher taxes. And if we are able to slow the growth of health care costs by just one-tenth of 1 percent each year -- one-tenth of 1 percent -- it will actually reduce the deficit by $4 trillion over the long term.

Now, this is the plan I'm proposing. It's a plan that incorporates ideas from many of the people in this room tonight -- Democrats and Republicans. And I will continue to seek common ground in the weeks ahead. If you come to me with a serious set of proposals, I will be there to listen. My door is always open.

But know this: I will not waste time with those who have made the calculation that it's better politics to kill this plan than to improve it. I won't stand by while the special interests use the same old tactics to keep things exactly the way they are. If you misrepresent what's in this plan, we will call you out. And I will not -- and I will not accept the status quo as a solution. Not this time. Not now.

Everyone in this room knows what will happen if we do nothing. Our deficit will grow. More families will go bankrupt. More businesses will close. More Americans will lose their coverage when they are sick

and need it the most. And more will die as a result.
We know these things to be true.

That is why we cannot fail. Because there are too
many Americans counting on us to succeed -- the
ones who suffer silently, and the ones who shared
their stories with us at town halls, in e-mails, and in
letters.

I received one of those letters a few days ago. It was
from our beloved friend and colleague, Ted Kennedy.
He had written it back in May, shortly after he was
told that his illness was terminal. He asked that it be
delivered upon his death.

In it, he spoke about what a happy time his last
months were, thanks to the love and support of
family and friends, his wife, Vicki, his amazing
children, who are all here tonight. And he expressed
confidence that this would be the year that health
care reform -- "that great unfinished business of our
society," he called it -- would finally pass. He
repeated the truth that health care is decisive for our
future prosperity, but he also reminded me that "it
concerns more than material things." "What we
face," he wrote, "is above all a moral issue; at stake
are not just the details of policy, but fundamental
principles of social justice and the character of our
country."

I've thought about that phrase quite a bit in recent
days -- the character of our country. One of the
unique and wonderful things about America has
always been our self-reliance, our rugged
individualism, our fierce defense of freedom and our

healthy skepticism of government. And figuring out
the appropriate size and role of government has
always been a source of rigorous and, yes, sometimes
angry debate. That's our history.
For some of Ted Kennedy's critics, his brand of
liberalism represented an affront to American liberty.
In their minds, his passion for universal health care
was nothing more than a passion for big government.

But those of us who knew Teddy and worked with
him here -- people of both parties -- know that
what drove him was something more. His friend
Orrin Hatch -- he knows that. They worked together
to provide children with health insurance. His friend
John McCain knows that. They worked together on a
Patient's Bill of Rights. His friend Chuck Grassley
knows that. They worked together to provide health
care to children with disabilities.
On issues like these, Ted Kennedy's passion was born
not of some rigid ideology, but of his own experience.
It was the experience of having two children stricken
with cancer. He never forgot the sheer terror and
helplessness that any parent feels when a child is
badly sick. And he was able to imagine what it must
be like for those without insurance, what it would be
like to have to say to a wife or a child or an aging
parent, there is something that could make you
better, but I just can't afford it.

That large-heartedness -- that concern and regard
for the plight of others -- is not a partisan feeling.
It's not a Republican or a Democratic feeling. It, too,
is part of the American character -- our ability to
stand in other people's shoes; a recognition that we
are all in this together, and when fortune turns

against one of us, others are there to lend a helping hand; a belief that in this country, hard work and responsibility should be rewarded by some measure of security and fair play; and an acknowledgment that sometimes government has to step in to help deliver on that promise.

This has always been the history of our progress. In 1935, when over half of our seniors could not support themselves and millions had seen their savings wiped away, there were those who argued that Social Security would lead to socialism, but the men and women of Congress stood fast, and we are all the better for it. In 1965, when some argued that Medicare represented a government takeover of health care, members of Congress -- Democrats and Republicans -- did not back down. They joined together so that all of us could enter our golden years with some basic peace of mind.

You see, our predecessors understood that government could not, and should not, solve every problem. They understood that there are instances when the gains in security from government action are not worth the added constraints on our freedom. But they also understood that the danger of too much government is matched by the perils of too little; that without the leavening hand of wise policy, markets can crash, monopolies can stifle competition, the vulnerable can be exploited. And they knew that when any government measure, no matter how carefully crafted or beneficial, is subject to scorn; when any efforts to help people in need are attacked as un-American; when facts and reason are thrown overboard and only timidity passes for wisdom, and we can no longer even engage in a civil conversation with each other over the things that truly matter -- that at that point we don't merely lose our capacity to solve big challenges. We lose something essential about ourselves.

That was true then. It remains true today. I understand how difficult this health care debate has been. I know that many in this country are deeply skeptical that government is looking out for them. I understand that the politically safe move would be to kick the can further down the road -- to defer reform one more year, or one more election, or one more term.

But that is not what the moment calls for. That's not what we came here to do. We did not come to fear the future. We came here to shape it. I still believe we can act even when it's hard. I still believe -- I still believe that we can act when it's hard. I still believe we can replace acrimony with civility, and gridlock with progress. I still believe we can do great things, and that here and now we will meet history's test.

Because that's who we are. That is our calling. That is our character. Thank you, God bless you, and may God bless the United States of America.

5 "You didn't build that."

July 13, 2012
Roanoke, Virginia

2012 election campaign speech reflecting the belief that successful citizens owe their success partly to public infrastructure and government spending, and that they should contribute to finance public goods.

Now, let me just say, unless you have managed to break your television set -- you're probably aware that it is campaign season. And I know it's not always pretty to watch. We're seeing more money flooding into the system than ever before, more negative ads, more cynicism. A lot of the reporting is just about who's up and who's down in the polls instead of talking about the things that matter in your day-to-day life.

So I know all this kind of makes it tempting to just turn off the TV set, and turn away from politics. And there are some people who are betting that you lose interest.

AUDIENCE: No!

But the fact that you are here tells me that you're still ready to work to make this a better country. You're still betting on hope and you're still betting on change -- and I am still betting on you.

AUDIENCE MEMBER: We love you, Mr. President!

I love you back.

AUDIENCE: Four more years! Four more years!

Well, let me just say this -- if I win Virginia, I'm going to get four more years. That I can say with some confidence.

And the reason you're here tonight is because no matter how petty and small politics seems sometimes, you recognize that the stakes could not be bigger. In some ways, the stakes are even bigger now than they were in 2008, because what's at stake is not just two people or two political parties. What's at stake is a decision between two fundamentally different views about where we take the country right now. And the choice is up to you. Now, this is my last political campaign.

AUDIENCE MEMBER: Awww --

No, it's true. There is a term limit for Presidents. You get two. So no matter what happens, this will be my last campaign. And it makes you nostalgic sometimes, and I started thinking about some of my first campaigns.

When I was traveling across Illinois -- and Illinois is a big state. And it's got big cities like Chicago and it's got small towns, and it's got rural areas and suburban areas, and you meet people from every walk of life -- black, white, Latino, Asian, Native American. You stop in VFW halls, you stop in diners, you go to churches, you go to synagogues. Wherever you go, you're going to have a chance to meet people from different walks of life. And when I think about that first campaign, what strikes me is no matter where I went, no matter who I was talking to, I could see my own life in the life of the people whose vote I was asking for.

So I would meet an elderly vet and I'd think about my grandfather who fought in World War II, and my grandmother who worked on a bomber assembly line during the war. And I'd think about how, when my grandfather came back home, because of this country he was able to get an education on the GI Bill and they were able to buy their first home using an FHA loan.

And then I'd meet a single mom somewhere and I'd think about my mom. I never knew my dad. He left when I was just barely a baby, and so -- and my mother didn't have a lot of money and she was struggling, and she had to go back to school raising a kid, later raising my sister, and she had to work while she was in school. But despite all that, because she was in America, she was able to get grants and scholarships and her kids were able to get grants and scholarships. And they could go as far as their dreams could take them.

And then I'd talk to some working folks, and I'd think about Michelle's family -- her dad who was a blue-collar worker, worked at a water filtration plant in Chicago, and her mom was a secretary. And yet, despite never having a lot, there was so much love and so much passion -- and her dad had MS, so he had to wake up an hour earlier than everybody else just to get to work because it took him that long to get dressed, and he could barely walk. But he never missed a day's work -- because he took pride in the idea that, you know what, I'm going to earn my way and look after my family. And I'd see that same pride in the people I was talking to.

And what this reminded me of was that, at the heart of this country, its central idea is the idea that in this country, if you're willing to work hard, if you're willing to take responsibility, you can make it if you try. That you can find a job that supports a family and find a home you can make your own; that you won't go bankrupt when you get sick. That maybe you can take a little vacation with your family once in a while -- nothing fancy, but just time to spend with those you love. Maybe see the country a little bit, maybe come down to Roanoke. That your kids can get a great education, and if they're willing to work hard, then they can achieve things that you wouldn't have even imagined achieving. And then you can maybe retire with some dignity and some respect, and be part of a community and give something back.

That's the idea of America. It doesn't matter what you look like. It doesn't matter where you come from. It doesn't matter what your last name is. You can live out the American Dream. That's what binds us all together.

Now, the reason that I think so many of us came together in 2008 was because we saw that for a decade that dream was fraying, that it was slipping away; that there were too many people who were working hard but not seeing their incomes or wages go up; that we had taken a surplus and turned it into a deficit -- we were running two wars on a credit card; that job growth was the most sluggish it had been in 50 years. There was a sense that those who were in charge didn't feel responsible.

And so we came together to say we are going to bring about the kinds of changes that allow us to get back to those basics, allow us to restore and live out those values. What we didn't realize was that some of that recklessness, some of that irresponsibility would lead to the worst financial crisis we've seen since the Great Depression. And I don't need to tell you what we've been through over the last three and a half years because you've lived it. Too many folks lost jobs. Too many people saw their homes lose value. Too many folks saw their savings take a hit.

But you know what's given me confidence and faith is that fact that as I've traveled around the country now, just like I used to travel around Illinois, that same decency, those same values -- they're still alive, at least outside Washington. Times have been tough, but America's character hasn't changed. The core decency of the American people is undiminished. Our willingness to fight through and work through the tough times and come together, that's still there.

And so, just as we came together in the last campaign -- not just Democrats, by the way, but Republicans and independents, because we're not Democrats or Republicans first, we're Americans first. Just like we came together in 2008, we know that we've got to keep working, we got to keep moving forward in 2012. And we knew back then that it wasn't going to be easy. These problems we're facing, they didn't happen overnight, and they're not going to be solved overnight. We understood it might take more than one year or one term or even one President. But what we also understood was that we weren't going to stop until we had restored that basic American bargain that makes us the greatest country on Earth.

Our goal isn't just to put people back to work -- although that's priority number one -- it is to build an economy where that work pays off. An economy where everyone, whether you are starting a business or punching a clock, can see your hard work and responsibility rewarded. That's what this campaign's about, Roanoke. And that's why I'm running for a second term as President of the United States of America.

AUDIENCE: Four more years! Four more years!

Now, let me say this. It's fashionable among some pundits -- and this happens every time America hits a rough patch -- it's fashionable to be saying, well, this time it's different, this time we really are in the soup; it's going to be hard to solve our problems. Let me tell you something. What's missing is not big ideas. What's missing is not that we've got an absence of technical solutions to deal with issues like education or energy or our deficit. The problem we've got right now is we've just got a stalemate in Washington.

And the outcome of this debate that we're having is going to set the stage not just for the next year or five years, but for the next twenty. On the one side you've got my opponent in this presidential race and his Republican allies who --

AUDIENCE: Booo --

No, no, look -- I mean, we're having a good, healthy, democratic debate. That's how this works. And on their side, they've got a basic theory about how you grow the economy. And the theory is very simple: They think that the economy grows from the top down. So their basic theory is, if wealthy investors are doing well then everybody does well. So if we spend trillions of dollars on more tax cuts mostly for the wealthy, that that's somehow going to create jobs, even if we have to pay for it by gutting education and gutting job-training programs and gutting transportation projects, and maybe even seeing middle-class folks have a higher tax burden.

AUDIENCE: No!

So that's part number one, right. More tax cuts for those at the top.

Part number two is they believe if you tear down all the regulations that we've put in place -- for example, on Wall Street banks, or on insurance, companies or on credit card companies, or on polluters -- that somehow the economy is going to do much, much better. So those are their two theories. They've got the tax cuts for the high end, and they've got rollback regulation.

Now, here's the problem. You may have guessed -- we tried this. We tried this in the last decade and it did not work.

AUDIENCE: No!

Now, before I finish, can I say, by the way, that some of you have been standing for a while and I see a couple folks slumping down a little bit. Make sure you're drinking water. Bend your knees. Don't stand up too straight. The paralegals will be -- the paralegals? You don't need lawyers. The paramedics will be coming by, so just give folks a little bit of room, they'll be fine. This happens at every event.

AUDIENCE MEMBER: We love you, Obama!

I love you back. But I just want to point out that we tried their theory for almost 10 years, and here's what it got us: We got the slowest job growth in decades. We got deficits as far as the eye can see. Your incomes and your wages didn't go up. And it culminated in a crisis because there weren't enough regulations on Wall Street and they could make reckless bets with other people's money that resulted in this financial crisis, and you had to foot the bill. So that's where their theory turned out.

Now, we don't need more top-down economics. I've got a different view. I believe that the way you grow the economy is from the middle out. I believe that you grow the economy from the bottom up. I believe that when working people are doing well, the country does well.

I believe in fighting for the middle class because if they're prospering, all of us will prosper. That's what I'm fighting for, and that's why I'm running for a second term as President of the United States.

Now, this is what I've been focused on since I've been in office. In 2008, I promised to make sure that middle-class taxes didn't go up. And in fact, because of the recession, you needed some help, so we cut the typical family's income taxes by $3,600. So if you hear somebody say that I'm a big tax guy, just remember $3,600 for the typical family. That's the tax break you've gotten since I've been in office.

Four years later, I'm running to keep middle-class taxes low. So this week, I called on Congress to immediately extend income tax cuts on the first $250,000 of income. Now, what that means is 98 percent of Americans make less than $250,000, so 98 percent of folks would have the certainty and security that your taxes, your income taxes would not go up a dime. And, by the way, this is not a hypothetical. This wasn't some campaign promise. The reason I called on Congress to act now is because if they don't do anything, on January 1st, almost everybody here, your taxes will go up an average of $1,600.

AUDIENCE: Booo --

So we need to stop that tax hike from happening. So you would think that this makes sense, right, because the Republicans say they're the party of no new taxes, right? That's what they always say. Except so far, they've refused to act. And this might confuse you. You might say, why would they not want to give 98 percent of Americans the certainty of this income tax cut?

Well, it turns out they don't want you to get your tax break unless the other 2 percent, the top 2 percent, they get their tax break as well.

Now, understand, the top 2 percent, folks like me, we're the ones who most benefited over the last decade from not only tax breaks, but also a lot of the money from increased profits and productivity went up to that top 2 percent. So the bottom line is, the top 2 percent doesn't need help. They're doing just fine.

And I understand why they wouldn't want to pay more in taxes. Nobody likes to pay more in taxes. Here's the problem: If you continue their tax breaks, that costs a trillion dollars. And since we're trying to bring down our deficit and our debt, if we spend a trillion dollars on tax cuts for them, we're going to have to find that trillion dollars someplace else. That means we're going to have to maybe make student loans more expensive for students. Or we might have to cut back on the services we're providing our brave veterans when they come home.

AUDIENCE: No!

Or we might have to stop investing in basic science and research that keeps us as a leading-edge economy. Or, as they suggested, maybe you would have to turn Medicare into a voucher program.

AUDIENCE: No!

I don't think those are good ideas. So what I've said to the Republicans is, look, all right, let's have this debate about the tax cuts for the wealthiest folks. I don't mind having that debate. But in the meantime, let's go ahead and do what we agree on, which is give 98 percent of Americans some certainty and some security. So far, they haven't taken me up on my offer.

Now, this gives you a sense of how Congress works these days -- you've got the possibility of your taxes going up in four months, five months, and instead of working on that, guess what they worked on this week? They worked --

AUDIENCE MEMBER: Nothing!

-- they voted for the 33rd time to try to repeal a health care bill we passed two years ago, after the Supreme Court said it's constitutional and we are going to go ahead and implement that law. I don't know about you, Virginia, but I think they've got a better way to use their time. I think helping you make sure your taxes don't go up, that would be a good use of congressional time.

Now, this is just a small example of the difference

between myself and Mr. Romney, between myself and some of the Republicans who are running Congress. And look, Virginia, I want to repeat -- this is a choice. If you think their way of doing things is a recipe for economic growth and helping the middle class, then you should vote for them.

AUDIENCE: No!

You can send those folks to Washington. I promise you they will carry out what they promise to do.

But that's not why I went to Washington. I went to Washington to fight for the middle class. I went to Washington to fight for working people who are trying to get into the middle class, and have some sense of security in their lives. People like me and Mr. Romney don't need another tax cut. You need some help right now to make sure your kids are living the kind of life you want for them. And that's why I'm running for a second term as President of the United States.

On almost every issue, you've got the same kind of choice. When the auto industry was about to go under, a million jobs lost, and my opponent said, "let's let Detroit go bankrupt," what did I say? I said --

AUDIENCE: No!

I said I'm betting on America's workers. I'm betting on American industry. And guess what? Three years later, GM is number one again and the American auto industry has come roaring back.

So I believe in American manufacturing. I believe in making stuff here in America. My opponent, he invested in companies who are called "pioneers" of outsourcing. I don't believe in outsourcing -- I believe in insourcing. I want to stop giving tax breaks to companies that ship jobs overseas; let's give tax breaks to companies that are investing right here in Roanoke, right here in the United States of America. Let's invest in American workers so they can make products and ship them around the world with those three proud words: Made in America.

I'm running because our men and women in uniform have sacrificed so much. We could not be prouder of them and we could not be prouder of our veterans. And because of their efforts, I was able to keep my promise and end the war in Iraq.

And I now intend to transition out of Afghanistan and bring our troops home. And what I said is, because of their outstanding work, we've been able to decimate al Qaeda and take out bin Laden. And so now it's time for us to take half of the money we were saving on war and pay down our deficit, and use the other half to do some nation-building here at home.

Roanoke knows something about transportation -- this was a railroad hub for a long time. So you know how important that is to growing an economy. Let's take some of that money and rebuild our roads and our bridges and our rail systems, and let's build wireless networks into rural communities so everybody can tap into world markets. Let's put construction workers back to work doing what they do best and that is rebuilding America. That's why I'm running for a second term as President of the United States. That's the choice you face.

I'm running to make sure that our kids are getting the best education in the world. When I came into office, we passed a tuition tax credit that has saved millions of families thousands of dollars, and now I want to extend it. But I don't want to stop there. We just won a fight thanks to some of the folks who are here, including students from VT that -- we just won a fight to make sure that student loan interest rates would not double.

But that's not enough. I want to lower tuition to make it more affordable for all young people. I want to help our elementary schools and our middle schools and our high schools hire more teachers, especially in math and science. I want 2 million more people to be able to go to community colleges to get trained in the jobs that businesses are hiring for right now -- because a higher education, a good education is not a luxury, it is an economic necessity. That's how we're going to win the race for the future. And that's why I'm running for a second term as President -- to finish the job we started in 2008.

We've got to deal with homeownership, and the fact of the matter is that my opponent's philosophy when it comes to dealing with homeowners is, let the market bottom out and let as many foreclosures happen as it takes. I don't think that's part of a solution -- that's part of the problem.

So what I want to do is, I want to let every single

person refinance their homes and save about $3,000 a year because you'll spend that $3,000 on some of these stores right here in downtown. You'll help small businesses and large businesses grow because they'll have more customers. It will be good for you and it will be good for the economy. And that's why I'm running for a second term as President -- because I want to help America's homeowners.

I am running because I still believe that you shouldn't go bankrupt when you get sick. We passed that health care law because it was the right thing to do. And because we did, 30 million people who don't have health insurance are going to get help getting health insurance. Six million young people who didn't have health insurance can now stay on their parent's plan and get health insurance.

Seniors are seeing their prescription drug costs go down. And, by the way, if you've got health insurance, you're not getting hit by a tax. The only thing that's happening to you is that you now have more security because insurance companies can't drop you when you get sick. And they can't mess around with you because of some fine print in your policy. If you're paying your policy, you will get the deal that you paid for. That's why we passed health care reform.

Now, one last thing -- one of the biggest differences is how we pay down our debt and our deficit. My opponent, Mr. Romney's plan is he wants to cut taxes another $5 trillion on top of the Bush tax cuts.

AUDIENCE: Booo --

Well, first of all, like I said, the only way you can pay for that -- if you're actually saying you're bringing down the deficit -- is to cut transportation, cut education, cut basic research, voucherize Medicare, and you're still going to end up having to raise taxes on middle-class families to pay for this $5 trillion tax cut. That's not a deficit reduction plan. That's a deficit expansion plan.

I've got a different idea. I do believe we can cut -- we've already made a trillion dollars' worth of cuts. We can make some more cuts in programs that don't work, and make government work more efficiently. Not every government program works the way it's supposed to. And frankly, government can't solve every problem. If somebody doesn't want to be helped, government can't always help them. Parents -- we can put more money into schools, but if your kids don't want to learn it's hard to teach them.

But you know what, I'm not going to see us gut the investments that grow our economy to give tax breaks to me or Mr. Romney or folks who don't need them. So I'm going to reduce the deficit in a balanced way. We've already made a trillion dollars' worth of cuts. We can make another trillion or trillion-two, and what we then do is ask for the wealthy to pay a little bit more. And, by the way, we've tried that before -- a guy named Bill Clinton did it. We created 23 million new jobs, turned a deficit into a surplus, and rich people did just fine. We created a lot of millionaires.

There are a lot of wealthy, successful Americans who

agree with me -- because they want to give something back. They know they didn't -- look, if you've been successful, you didn't get there on your own. You didn't get there on your own. I'm always struck by people who think, well, it must be because I was just so smart. There are a lot of smart people out there. It must be because I worked harder than everybody else. Let me tell you something -- there are a whole bunch of hardworking people out there.

If you were successful, somebody along the line gave you some help. There was a great teacher somewhere in your life. Somebody helped to create this unbelievable American system that we have that allowed you to thrive. Somebody invested in roads and bridges. If you've got a business -- you didn't build that. Somebody else made that happen. The Internet didn't get invented on its own. Government research created the Internet so that all the companies could make money off the Internet.

The point is, is that when we succeed, we succeed because of our individual initiative, but also because we do things together. There are some things, just like fighting fires, we don't do on our own. I mean, imagine if everybody had their own fire service. That would be a hard way to organize fighting fires.

So we say to ourselves, ever since the founding of this country, you know what, there are some things we do better together. That's how we funded the GI Bill. That's how we created the middle class. That's how we built the Golden Gate Bridge or the Hoover Dam. That's how we invented the Internet. That's how we sent a man to the moon. We rise or fall together as one nation and as one people, and that's the reason I'm running for President -- because I still believe in that idea. You're not on your own, we're in this together.

So all these issues go back to that first campaign that I talked about, because everything has to do with how do we help middle-class families, working people, strivers, doers -- how do we help them succeed? How do we make sure that their hard work pays off? That's what I've been thinking about the entire time I've been President.

Now, over the next four months, the other side is going to spend more money than we've even seen in history. And they don't really have a good argument for how they would do better, but they're thinking they can win the election if they just remind people that a lot of people are still out of work, and the economy is not growing as fast as it needs to, and it's all Obama's fault. That's basically their pitch.

AUDIENCE: Booo --

No, no, I mean, I'm just telling you. You've seen the ads, and they're going to run more of them, and there will be all kinds of variations on the same theme. But it will be the same basic message over and over and over and over and over again.

Now, their ads may be a plan to win an election, but it's not a plan to put people back to work. It's not a plan to strengthen the middle class. And the reason it doesn't worry me is because we've been outspent before. We've been counted out before. The pundits, they didn't think I could win Virginia the last time. The last time I came to this part of Virginia, all the political writers, they're all like, well, he's not serious, he's just making a tactical move. No, I'm serious -- I'm going to get some votes down here.

And so the reason that I continue to have confidence is because when I look at you, I see my grandparents. When I see your kids, I see my kids. And I think about all those previous generations -- our parents and grandparents and great-grandparents. Some of them came here as immigrants, some were brought here against their will. Some of them worked on farms, and some worked in mills, and some worked in mines, and some worked on the railroad.

But no matter where they worked, no matter how times were tough, they always had faith that there was something different about this country; that in this country, you have some God-given rights: a life in liberty and the pursuit of happiness, and a belief that all of us are equal -- and that we're not guaranteed success, but we're guaranteed the right to work hard for success.

They understood that, and they understood that succeeding in America wasn't about how much money was in your bank account, but it was about whether you were doing right by your people, doing right by your family, doing right by your neighborhood, doing right by your community, doing right by your country, living out our values, living out our dreams, living out our hopes. That's what America was about.

And so when I look out at this crowd, you inspire me. And I have to tell you that the privilege of being your President is something that I thank God for every single day.

I said to you back in 2008 when I was running, I'm not a perfect man -- you can ask Michelle about that. And I told you I wouldn't be a perfect President. But what I did say to you was that I'd always tell you what I thought and I'd always tell you where I stood, and that I would wake up every single morning thinking about you and fighting as hard as I knew how to make your life a little bit better.

And over these last three and a half years, I know times have been tough, and I know change hasn't always come as fast as you'd like. But you know what, I've kept that promise. I thought about you. I fought for you. I believe in you. And if you still believe in me, if you're willing to stand up with me, and campaign with me, and make phone calls for me, and knock on doors with me, I promise you we will finish what we started -- and we will restore that basic bargain that built this country, and we'll remind the world just why it is that America is the greatest nation on Earth.

God bless you, and God bless the United States of America.

6 "On Monday morning, the sun rose over Boston."

Interfaith Service for the Victims of the Boston Bombing
April 18, 2013

Hello, Boston!

Scripture tells us to "run with endurance the race that is set before us." Run with endurance the race that is set before us.

On Monday morning, the sun rose over Boston. The sunlight glistened off the Statehouse dome. In the Common and the Public Garden, spring was in bloom. On this Patriot's Day, like so many before, fans jumped onto the T to see the Sox at Fenway. In Hopkinton, runners laced up their shoes and set out on a 26.2-mile test of dedication and grit and the human spirit. And across this city, hundreds of thousands of Bostonians lined the streets -- to hand the runners cups of water and to cheer them on.

It was a beautiful day to be in Boston -- a day that explains why a poet once wrote that this town is not just a capital, not just a place. Boston, he said, "is the perfect state of grace."

And then, in an instant, the day's beauty was shattered. A celebration became a tragedy. And so we come together to pray, and mourn, and measure our loss. But we also come together today to reclaim that state of grace -- to reaffirm that the spirit of this city is undaunted, and the spirit of this country shall remain undimmed.

To Governor Patrick; Mayor Menino; Cardinal O'Malley and all the faith leaders who are here; Governors Romney, Swift, Weld and Dukakis; members of Congress; and most of all, the people of Boston and the families who've lost a piece of your heart. We thank you for your leadership. We thank you for your courage. We thank you for your grace.

I'm here today on behalf of the American people with a simple message: Every one of us has been touched by this attack on your beloved city. Every one of us stands with you.

Because, after all, it's our beloved city, too. Boston may be your hometown, but we claim it, too. It's one of America's iconic cities. It's one of the world's great cities. And one of the reasons the world knows Boston so well is that Boston opens its heart to the world.

Over successive generations, you've welcomed again

and again new arrivals to our shores -- immigrants who constantly reinvigorated this city and this commonwealth and our nation. Every fall, you welcome students from all across America and all across the globe, and every spring you graduate them back into the world -- a Boston diaspora that excels in every field of human endeavor. Year after year, you welcome the greatest talents in the arts and science, research -- you welcome them to your concert halls and your hospitals and your laboratories to exchange ideas and insights that draw this world together.

And every third Monday in April, you welcome people from all around the world to the Hub for friendship and fellowship and healthy competition -- a gathering of men and women of every race and every religion, every shape and every size; a multitude represented by all those flags that flew over the finish line.

So whether folks come here to Boston for just a day, or they stay here for years, they leave with a piece of this town tucked firmly into their hearts. So Boston is your hometown, but we claim it a little bit, too.

I know this because there's a piece of Boston in me. You welcomed me as a young law student across the river; welcomed Michelle, too. You welcomed me during a convention when I was still a state senator and very few people could pronounce my name right.

Like you, Michelle and I have walked these streets. Like you, we know these neighborhoods. And like you, in this moment of grief, we join you in saying --

"Boston, you're my home." For millions of us, what happened on Monday is personal. It's personal.

Today our prayers are with the Campbell family of Medford. They're here today. Their daughter, Krystle, was always smiling. Those who knew her said that with her red hair and her freckles and her ever-eager willingness to speak her mind, she was beautiful, sometimes she could be a little noisy, and everybody loved her for it. She would have turned 30 next month. As her mother said through her tears, "This doesn't make any sense."

Our prayers are with the Lu family of China, who sent their daughter, Lingzi, to BU so that she could experience all this city has to offer. She was a 23-year-old student, far from home. And in the heartache of her family and friends on both sides of a great ocean, we're reminded of the humanity that we all share.

Our prayers are with the Richard family of Dorchester -- to Denise and their young daughter, Jane, as they fight to recover. And our hearts are broken for 8-year-old Martin -- with his big smile and bright eyes. His last hours were as perfect as an 8-year-old boy could hope for -- with his family, eating ice cream at a sporting event. And we're left with two enduring images of this little boy -- forever smiling for his beloved Bruins, and forever expressing a wish he made on a blue poster board: "No more hurting people. Peace."

No more hurting people. Peace.

Our prayers are with the injured --- so many wounded, some gravely. From their beds, some are surely watching us gather here today. And if you are, know this: As you begin this long journey of recovery, your city is with you. Your commonwealth is with you. Your country is with you. We will all be with you as you learn to stand and walk and, yes, run again. Of that I have no doubt. You will run again. You will run again.

Because that's what the people of Boston are made of. Your resolve is the greatest rebuke to whoever committed this heinous act. If they sought to intimidate us, to terrorize us, to shake us from those values that Deval described, the values that make us who we are, as Americans -- well, it should be pretty clear by now that they picked the wrong city to do it. Not here in Boston. Not here in Boston.

You've shown us, Boston, that in the face of evil, Americans will lift up what's good. In the face of cruelty, we will choose compassion. In the face of those who would visit death upon innocents, we will choose to save and to comfort and to heal. We'll choose friendship. We'll choose love.

Scripture teaches us, "God has not given us a spirit of fear and timidity, but of power, love, and self-discipline." And that's the spirit you've displayed in recent days.

When doctors and nurses, police and firefighters and EMTs and Guardsmen run towards explosions to treat the wounded -- that's discipline.

When exhausted runners, including our troops and veterans -- who never expected to see such carnage on the streets back home -- become first responders themselves, tending to the injured -- that's real power.

When Bostonians carry victims in their arms, deliver water and blankets, line up to give blood, open their homes to total strangers, give them rides back to reunite with their families -- that's love.

That's the message we send to those who carried this out and anyone who would do harm to our people. Yes, we will find you. And, yes, you will face justice. We will find you. We will hold you accountable. But more than that; our fidelity to our way of life -- to our free and open society -- will only grow stronger. For God has not given us a spirit of fear and timidity, but one of power and love and self-discipline.

Like Bill Iffrig, 78 years old -- the runner in the orange tank top who we all saw get knocked down by the blast -- we may be momentarily knocked off our feet, but we'll pick ourselves up. We'll keep going. We will finish the race. In the words of Dick Hoyt, who's pushed his disabled son, Rick, in 31 Boston Marathons -- "We can't let something like this stop us." This doesn't stop us.

And that's what you've taught us, Boston. That's what you've reminded us -- to push on. To persevere. To not grow weary. To not get faint. Even when it hurts. Even when our heart aches. We summon the strength that maybe we didn't even know we had, and we carry on. We finish the race.

We finish the race.

And we do that because of who we are. And we do that because we know that somewhere around the bend a stranger has a cup of water. Around the bend, somebody is there to boost our spirits. On that toughest mile, just when we think that we've hit a wall, someone will be there to cheer us on and pick us up if we fall. We know that.

And that's what the perpetrators of such senseless violence -- these small, stunted individuals who would destroy instead of build, and think somehow that makes them important -- that's what they don't understand. Our faith in each other, our love for each other, our love for country, our common creed that cuts across whatever superficial differences there may be -- that is our power. That's our strength.

That's why a bomb can't beat us. That's why we don't hunker down. That's why we don't cower in fear. We carry on. We race. We strive. We build, and we work, and we love -- and we raise our kids to do the same. And we come together to celebrate life, and to walk our cities, and to cheer for our teams. When the Sox and Celtics and Patriots or Bruins are champions again -- to the chagrin of New York and Chicago fans -- the crowds will gather and watch a parade go down Boylston Street.

And this time next year, on the third Monday in April, the world will return to this great American city to run harder than ever, and to cheer even louder, for the 118th Boston Marathon. Bet on it.

Tomorrow, the sun will rise over Boston. Tomorrow, the sun will rise over this country that we love. This special place. This state of grace.

Scripture tells us to "run with endurance the race that is set before us." As we do, may God hold close those who've been taken from us too soon. May He comfort their families. And may He continue to watch over these United States of America.

7 "It was not a clash of armies, but a clash of wills."

50th Anniversary of the Selma to Montgomery Marches
March 7, 2015
Edmund Pettus Bridge, Selma, Alabama.

Delivered at Edmund Pettus Bridge to mark the 50th anniversary of the Selma to Montgomery marches. Among the estimated 40,000 present were former President George W. Bush, former First Lady Laura Bush, and Amelia Boynton Robinson, John Lewis, Diane Nash, Bernard Lafayette, and many other 'foot soldiers' who had taken part in the march in 1965.

It is a rare honor in this life to follow one of your heroes. And John Lewis is one of my heroes.

Now, I have to imagine that when a younger John Lewis woke up that morning 50 years ago and made his way to Brown Chapel, heroics were not on his mind. A day like this was not on his mind. Young folks with bedrolls and backpacks were milling about. Veterans of the movement trained newcomers in the tactics of non-violence; the right way to protect yourself when attacked. A doctor described what tear gas does to the body, while marchers scribbled down instructions for contacting their loved ones. The air was thick with doubt, anticipation and fear. And they comforted themselves with the final verse of the final hymn they sung:

"No matter what may be the test, God will take care of you;
Lean, weary one, upon His breast, God will take care of you."

And then, his knapsack stocked with an apple, a toothbrush, and a book on government -- all you need for a night behind bars -- John Lewis led them out of the church on a mission to change America.

President and Mrs. Bush, Governor Bentley, Mayor Evans, Sewell, Reverend Strong, members of Congress, elected officials, foot soldiers, friends, fellow Americans:

As John noted, there are places and moments in America where this nation's destiny has been decided. Many are sites of war -- Concord and Lexington, Appomattox, Gettysburg. Others are sites that symbolize the daring of America's character -- Independence Hall and Seneca Falls, Kitty Hawk and Cape Canaveral.

Selma is such a place. In one afternoon 50 years ago, so much of our turbulent history -- the stain of slavery and anguish of civil war; the yoke of segregation and tyranny of Jim Crow; the death of four little girls in Birmingham; and the dream of a Baptist preacher -- all that history met on this bridge.

It was not a clash of armies, but a clash of wills; a contest to determine the true meaning of America. And because of men and women like John Lewis, Joseph Lowery, Hosea Williams, Amelia Boynton, Diane Nash, Ralph Abernathy, C.T. Vivian, Andrew Young, Fred Shuttlesworth, Dr. Martin Luther King, Jr., and so many others, the idea of a just America and a fair America, an inclusive America, and a generous America -- that idea ultimately triumphed.

As is true across the landscape of American history, we cannot examine this moment in isolation. The march on Selma was part of a broader campaign that spanned generations; the leaders that day part of a long line of heroes.

We gather here to celebrate them. We gather here to honor the courage of ordinary Americans willing to endure billy clubs and the chastening rod; tear gas and the trampling hoof; men and women who despite the gush of blood and splintered bone would stay true to their North Star and keep marching towards justice.

They did as Scripture instructed: "Rejoice in hope, be patient in tribulation, be constant in prayer." And in the days to come, they went back again and again. When the trumpet call sounded for more to join, the people came -- black and white, young and old,

Christian and Jew, waving the American flag and singing the same anthems full of faith and hope. A white newsman, Bill Plante, who covered the marches then and who is with us here today, quipped that the growing number of white people lowered the quality of the singing. To those who marched, though, those old gospel songs must have never sounded so sweet.

In time, their chorus would well up and reach President Johnson. And he would send them protection, and speak to the nation, echoing their call for America and the world to hear: "We shall overcome." What enormous faith these men and women had. Faith in God, but also faith in America.

The Americans who crossed this bridge, they were not physically imposing. But they gave courage to millions. They held no elected office. But they led a nation. They marched as Americans who had endured hundreds of years of brutal violence, countless daily indignities –– but they didn't seek special treatment, just the equal treatment promised to them almost a century before.

What they did here will reverberate through the ages. Not because the change they won was preordained; not because their victory was complete; but because they proved that nonviolent change is possible, that love and hope can conquer hate.

As we commemorate their achievement, we are well-served to remember that at the time of the marches, many in power condemned rather than praised them. Back then, they were called Communists, or half-breeds, or outside agitators, sexual and moral degenerates, and worse -- they were called everything but the name their parents gave them. Their faith was questioned. Their lives were threatened. Their patriotism challenged.

And yet, what could be more American than what happened in this place? What could more profoundly vindicate the idea of America than plain and humble people -- unsung, the downtrodden, the dreamers not of high station, not born to wealth or privilege, not of one religious tradition but many, coming together to shape their country's course?

What greater expression of faith in the American experiment than this, what greater form of patriotism is there than the belief that America is not yet finished, that we are strong enough to be self-critical, that each successive generation can look upon our imperfections and decide that it is in our power to remake this nation to more closely align with our highest ideals?

That's why Selma is not some outlier in the American experience. That's why it's not a museum or a static monument to behold from a distance. It is instead the manifestation of a creed written into our founding documents: "We the People...in order to form a more perfect union." "We hold these truths to be self-evident, that all men are created equal."

These are not just words. They're a living thing, a call to action, a roadmap for citizenship and an insistence in the capacity of free men and women to shape our own destiny. For founders like Franklin and Jefferson, for leaders like Lincoln and FDR, the success of our experiment in self-government rested on engaging all of our citizens in this work. And that's what we celebrate here in Selma. That's what this movement was all about, one leg in our long journey toward freedom.

The American instinct that led these young men and women to pick up the torch and cross this bridge, that's the same instinct that moved patriots to choose revolution over tyranny. It's the same instinct that drew immigrants from across oceans and the Rio Grande; the same instinct that led women to reach for the ballot, workers to organize against an unjust status quo; the same instinct that led us to plant a flag at Iwo Jima and on the surface of the Moon.

It's the idea held by generations of citizens who believed that America is a constant work in progress; who believed that loving this country requires more than singing its praises or avoiding uncomfortable truths. It requires the occasional disruption, the willingness to speak out for what is right, to shake up the status quo. That's America.

That's what makes us unique. That's what cements our reputation as a beacon of opportunity. Young people behind the Iron Curtain would see Selma and eventually tear down that wall. Young people in Soweto would hear Bobby Kennedy talk about ripples of hope and eventually banish the scourge of apartheid. Young people in Burma went to prison rather than submit to military rule. They saw what John Lewis had done. From the streets of Tunis to the Maidan in Ukraine, this generation of young people can draw strength from this place, where the powerless could change the world's greatest power and push their leaders to expand the boundaries of freedom.

They saw that idea made real right here in Selma, Alabama. They saw that idea manifest itself here in America.

Because of campaigns like this, a Voting Rights Act was passed. Political and economic and social barriers came down. And the change these men and women wrought is visible here today in the presence of African Americans who run boardrooms, who sit on the bench, who serve in elected office from small towns to big cities; from the Congressional Black Caucus all the way to the Oval Office.

Because of what they did, the doors of opportunity swung open not just for black folks, but for every American. Women marched through those doors. Latinos marched through those doors. Asian Americans, gay Americans, Americans with disabilities -- they all came through those doors. Their endeavors gave the entire South the chance to rise again, not by reasserting the past, but by transcending the past.

What a glorious thing, Dr. King might say. And what a solemn debt we owe. Which leads us to ask, just how might we repay that debt?

First and foremost, we have to recognize that one day's commemoration, no matter how special, is not enough. If Selma taught us anything, it's that our work is never done. The American experiment in self-government gives work and purpose to each generation.

Selma teaches us, as well, that action requires that we shed our cynicism. For when it comes to the pursuit of justice, we can afford neither complacency nor despair.

Just this week, I was asked whether I thought the Department of Justice's Ferguson report shows that, with respect to race, little has changed in this country. And I understood the question; the report's narrative was sadly familiar. It evoked the kind of abuse and disregard for citizens that spawned the Civil Rights Movement. But I rejected the notion that nothing's changed. What happened in Ferguson may not be unique, but it's no longer endemic. It's no longer sanctioned by law or by custom. And before the Civil Rights Movement, it most surely was.

We do a disservice to the cause of justice by intimating that bias and discrimination are immutable, that racial division is inherent to America. If you think nothing's changed in the past 50 years, ask somebody who lived through the Selma or Chicago or Los Angeles of the 1950s. Ask the female CEO who once might have been assigned to the secretarial pool if nothing's changed. Ask your gay friend if it's easier to be out and proud in America now than it was thirty years ago. To deny this progress, this hard-won progress -- our progress -- would be to rob us of our own agency, our own capacity, our responsibility to do what we can to make America better.

Of course, a more common mistake is to suggest that Ferguson is an isolated incident; that racism is banished; that the work that drew men and women to Selma is now complete, and that whatever racial tensions remain are a consequence of those seeking to play the "race card" for their own purposes. We don't need the Ferguson report to know that's not true. We just need to open our eyes, and our ears, and our hearts to know that this nation's racial history still casts its long shadow upon us.

We know the march is not yet over. We know the race is not yet won. We know that reaching that blessed destination where we are judged, all of us, by the content of our character requires admitting as much, facing up to the truth. "We are capable of bearing a great burden," James Baldwin once wrote, "once we discover that the burden is reality and arrive where reality is."

There's nothing America can't handle if we actually look squarely at the problem. And this is work for all Americans, not just some. Not just whites. Not just blacks. If we want to honor the courage of those who marched that day, then all of us are called to possess their moral imagination. All of us will need to feel as they did the fierce urgency of now. All of us need to recognize as they did that change depends on our actions, on our attitudes, the things we teach our children. And if we make such an effort, no matter how hard it may sometimes seem, laws can be passed, and consciences can be stirred, and consensus can be built.

With such an effort, we can make sure our criminal justice system serves all and not just some.

Together, we can raise the level of mutual trust that policing is built on -- the idea that police officers are members of the community they risk their lives to protect, and citizens in Ferguson and New York and Cleveland, they just want the same thing young people here marched for 50 years ago -- the protection of the law.

Together, we can address unfair sentencing and overcrowded prisons, and the stunted circumstances that rob too many boys of the chance to become men, and rob the nation of too many men who could be good dads, and good workers, and good neighbors.

With effort, we can roll back poverty and the roadblocks to opportunity. Americans don't accept a free ride for anybody, nor do we believe in equality of outcomes. But we do expect equal opportunity. And if we really mean it, if we're not just giving lip service to it, but if we really mean it and are willing to sacrifice for it, then, yes, we can make sure every child gets an education suitable to this new century, one that expands imaginations and lifts sights and gives those children the skills they need. We can make sure every person willing to work has the dignity of a job, and a fair wage, and a real voice, and sturdier rungs on that ladder into the middle class.

And with effort, we can protect the foundation stone of our democracy for which so many marched across this bridge -- and that is the right to vote. Right now, in 2015, 50 years after Selma, there are laws across this country designed to make it harder for people to vote. As we speak, more of such laws are being proposed. Meanwhile, the Voting Rights Act, the culmination of so much blood, so much sweat and tears, the product of so much sacrifice in the face of wanton violence, the Voting Rights Act stands weakened, its future subject to political rancor.

How can that be? The Voting Rights Act was one of the crowning achievements of our democracy, the result of Republican and Democratic efforts. President Reagan signed its renewal when he was in office. President George W. Bush signed its renewal when he was in office. One hundred members of Congress have come here today to honor people who were willing to die for the right to protect it. If we want to honor this day, let that hundred go back to Washington and gather four hundred more, and together, pledge to make it their mission to restore that law this year. That's how we honor those on this bridge.

Of course, our democracy is not the task of Congress alone, or the courts alone, or even the President alone. If every new voter-suppression law was struck down today, we would still have, here in America, one of the lowest voting rates among free peoples. Fifty years ago, registering to vote here in Selma and much of the South meant guessing the number of jellybeans in a jar, the number of bubbles on a bar of soap. It meant risking your dignity, and sometimes, your life.

What's our excuse today for not voting? How do we

so casually discard the right for which so many fought? How do we so fully give away our power, our voice, in shaping America's future? Why are we pointing to somebody else when we could take the time just to go to the polling places? We give away our power.

Fellow marchers, so much has changed in 50 years. We have endured war and we've fashioned peace. We've seen technological wonders that touch every aspect of our lives. We take for granted conveniences that our parents could have scarcely imagined. But what has not changed is the imperative of citizenship; that willingness of a 26-year-old deacon, or a Unitarian minister, or a young mother of five to decide they loved this country so much that they'd risk everything to realize its promise.

That's what it means to love America. That's what it means to believe in America. That's what it means when we say America is exceptional.

For we were born of change. We broke the old aristocracies, declaring ourselves entitled not by bloodline, but endowed by our Creator with certain inalienable rights. We secure our rights and responsibilities through a system of self-government, of and by and for the people. That's why we argue and fight with so much passion and conviction -- because we know our efforts matter. We know America is what we make of it.

Look at our history. We are Lewis and Clark and Sacajawea, pioneers who braved the unfamiliar, followed by a stampede of farmers and miners, and

entrepreneurs and hucksters. That's our spirit.
That's who we are.

We are Sojourner Truth and Fannie Lou Hamer,
women who could do as much as any man and then
some. And we're Susan B. Anthony, who shook the
system until the law reflected that truth. That is our
character.

We're the immigrants who stowed away on ships to
reach these shores, the huddled masses yearning to
breathe free -- Holocaust survivors, Soviet defectors,
the Lost Boys of Sudan. We're the hopeful strivers
who cross the Rio Grande because we want our kids
to know a better life. That's how we came to be.

We're the slaves who built the White House and the
economy of the South. We're the ranch hands and
cowboys who opened up the West, and countless
laborers who laid rail, and raised skyscrapers, and
organized for workers' rights.

We're the fresh-faced GIs who fought to liberate a
continent. And we're the Tuskeegee Airmen, and the
Navajo code-talkers, and the Japanese Americans
who fought for this country even as their own liberty
had been denied.

We're the firefighters who rushed into those
buildings on 9/11, the volunteers who signed up to
fight in Afghanistan and Iraq. We're the gay
Americans whose blood ran in the streets of San
Francisco and New York, just as blood ran down this
bridge.

We are storytellers, writers, poets, artists who abhor unfairness, and despise hypocrisy, and give voice to the voiceless, and tell truths that need to be told.

We're the inventors of gospel and jazz and blues, bluegrass and country, and hip-hop and rock and roll, and our very own sound with all the sweet sorrow and reckless joy of freedom.

We are Jackie Robinson, enduring scorn and spiked cleats and pitches coming straight to his head, and stealing home in the World Series anyway.

We are the people Langston Hughes wrote of who "build our temples for tomorrow, strong as we know how." We are the people Emerson wrote of, "who for truth and honor's sake stand fast and suffer long;" who are "never tired, so long as we can see far enough."

That's what America is. Not stock photos or airbrushed history, or feeble attempts to define some of us as more American than others. We respect the past, but we don't pine for the past. We don't fear the future; we grab for it. America is not some fragile thing. We are large, in the words of Whitman, containing multitudes. We are boisterous and diverse and full of energy, perpetually young in spirit. That's why someone like John Lewis at the ripe old age of 25 could lead a mighty march.

And that's what the young people here today and listening all across the country must take away from this day. You are America. Unconstrained by habit and convention. Unencumbered by what is, because you're ready to seize what ought to be.

For everywhere in this country, there are first steps to be taken, there's new ground to cover, there are more bridges to be crossed. And it is you, the young and fearless at heart, the most diverse and educated generation in our history, who the nation is waiting to follow.

Because Selma shows us that America is not the project of any one person. Because the single-most powerful word in our democracy is the word "We." "We The People." "We Shall Overcome." "Yes We Can." That word is owned by no one. It belongs to everyone. Oh, what a glorious task we are given, to continually try to improve this great nation of ours.

Fifty years from Bloody Sunday, our march is not yet finished, but we're getting closer. Two hundred and thirty-nine years after this nation's founding our union is not yet perfect, but we are getting closer. Our job's easier because somebody already got us through that first mile. Somebody already got us over that bridge.

When it feels the road is too hard, when the torch we've been passed feels too heavy, we will remember these early travelers, and draw strength from their example, and hold firmly the words of the prophet Isaiah: "Those who hope in the Lord will renew their strength. They will soar on [the] wings like eagles. They will run and not grow weary. They will walk and not be faint."

We honor those who walked so we could run. We

must run so our children soar. And we will not grow weary. For we believe in the power of an awesome God, and we believe in this country's sacred promise.

May He bless those warriors of justice no longer with us, and bless the United States of America. Thank you, everybody.

8 "We don't earn grace... But God gives it to us anyway."

Eulogy for Clementa Pinckney
June 26, 2015
College of Charleston, Charleston, South Carolina

Delivered at the College of Charleston, after the Charleston church shooting, during which state senator Clementa C. Pinckney and eight other victims were gunned down by a white supremacist.

Giving all praise and honor to God.

The Bible calls us to hope. To persevere, and have faith in things not seen.

"They were still living by faith when they died," Scripture tells us. "They did not receive the things promised; they only saw them and welcomed them from a distance, admitting that they were foreigners and strangers on Earth."

We are here today to remember a man of God who lived by faith. A man who believed in things not seen. A man who believed there were better days ahead, off in the distance. A man of service who persevered, knowing full well he would not receive all those things he was promised, because he believed his efforts would deliver a better life for those who followed.

To Jennifer, his beloved wife; to Eliana and Malana, his beautiful, wonderful daughters; to the Mother Emanuel family and the people of Charleston, the people of South Carolina.

I cannot claim to have the good fortune to know Reverend Pinckney well. But I did have the pleasure of knowing him and meeting him here in South Carolina, back when we were both a little bit younger. Back when I didn't have visible grey hair. The first thing I noticed was his graciousness, his smile, his reassuring baritone, his deceptive sense of humor -- all qualities that helped him wear so effortlessly a heavy burden of expectation.

Friends of his remarked this week that when Clementa Pinckney entered a room, it was like the future arrived; that even from a young age, folks knew he was special. Anointed. He was the progeny of a long line of the faithful -- a family of preachers who spread God's word, a family of protesters who sowed change to expand voting rights and desegregate the South. Clem heard their instruction, and he did not forsake their teaching.

He was in the pulpit by 13, pastor by 18, public

servant by 23. He did not exhibit any of the cockiness of youth, nor youth's insecurities; instead, he set an example worthy of his position, wise beyond his years, in his speech, in his conduct, in his love, faith, and purity.

As a senator, he represented a sprawling swath of the Lowcountry, a place that has long been one of the most neglected in America. A place still wracked by poverty and inadequate schools; a place where children can still go hungry and the sick can go without treatment. A place that needed somebody like Clem.

His position in the minority party meant the odds of winning more resources for his constituents were often long. His calls for greater equity were too often unheeded, the votes he cast were sometimes lonely. But he never gave up. He stayed true to his convictions. He would not grow discouraged. After a full day at the capitol, he'd climb into his car and head to the church to draw sustenance from his family, from his ministry, from the community that loved and needed him. There he would fortify his faith, and imagine what might be.

Reverend Pinckney embodied a politics that was neither mean, nor small. He conducted himself quietly, and kindly, and diligently. He encouraged progress not by pushing his ideas alone, but by seeking out your ideas, partnering with you to make things happen. He was full of empathy and fellow feeling, able to walk in somebody else's shoes and see through their eyes. No wonder one of his senate colleagues remembered Senator Pinckney as "the most gentle of the 46 of us -- the best of the 46 of us."

Clem was often asked why he chose to be a pastor and a public servant. But the person who asked probably didn't know the history of the AME church. As our brothers and sisters in the AME church know, we don't make those distinctions. "Our calling," Clem once said, "is not just within the walls of the congregation, but...the life and community in which our congregation resides."

He embodied the idea that our Christian faith demands deeds and not just words; that the "sweet hour of prayer" actually lasts the whole week long -- that to put our faith in action is more than individual salvation, it's about our collective salvation; that to feed the hungry and clothe the naked and house the homeless is not just a call for isolated charity but the imperative of a just society.

What a good man. Sometimes I think that's the best thing to hope for when you're eulogized -- after all the words and recitations and resumes are read, to just say someone was a good man.

You don't have to be of high station to be a good man. Preacher by 13. Pastor by 18. Public servant by 23. What a life Clementa Pinckney lived. What an example he set. What a model for his faith. And then to lose him at 41 -- slain in his sanctuary with eight wonderful members of his flock, each at different stages in life but bound together by a common commitment to God.

Cynthia Hurd. Susie Jackson. Ethel Lance. DePayne Middleton-Doctor. Tywanza Sanders. Daniel L. Simmons. Sharonda Coleman-Singleton. Myra Thompson. Good people. Decent people. God-fearing people. People so full of life and so full of kindness. People who ran the race, who persevered. People of great faith.

To the families of the fallen, the nation shares in your grief. Our pain cuts that much deeper because it happened in a church. The church is and always has been the center of African-American life -- a place to call our own in a too often hostile world, a sanctuary from so many hardships.

Over the course of centuries, black churches served as "hush harbors" where slaves could worship in safety; praise houses where their free descendants could gather and shout hallelujah -- rest stops for the weary along the Underground Railroad; bunkers for the foot soldiers of the Civil Rights Movement. They have been, and continue to be, community centers where we organize for jobs and justice; places of scholarship and network; places where children are loved and fed and kept out of harm's way, and told that they are beautiful and smart -- and taught that they matter. That's what happens in church.

That's what the black church means. Our beating heart. The place where our dignity as a people is inviolate. When there's no better example of this tradition than Mother Emanuel -- a church built by blacks seeking liberty, burned to the ground because its founder sought to end slavery, only to rise up again, a Phoenix from these ashes.

When there were laws banning all-black church gatherings, services happened here anyway, in defiance of unjust laws. When there was a righteous movement to dismantle Jim Crow, Dr. Martin Luther King, Jr. preached from its pulpit, and marches began from its steps. A sacred place, this church. Not just for blacks, not just for Christians, but for every American who cares about the steady expansion -- of human rights and human dignity in this country; a foundation stone for liberty and justice for all. That's what the church meant.

We do not know whether the killer of Reverend Pinckney and eight others knew all of this history. But he surely sensed the meaning of his violent act. It was an act that drew on a long history of bombs and arson and shots fired at churches, not random, but as a means of control, a way to terrorize and oppress. An act that he imagined would incite fear and recrimination; violence and suspicion. An act that he presumed would deepen divisions that trace back to our nation's original sin.

Oh, but God works in mysterious ways. God has different ideas.

He didn't know he was being used by God. Blinded by hatred, the alleged killer could not see the grace surrounding Reverend Pinckney and that Bible study group -- the light of love that shone as they opened the church doors and invited a stranger to join in their prayer circle. The alleged killer could have never anticipated the way the families of the fallen would respond when they saw him in court -- in the midst of unspeakable grief, with words of forgiveness. He couldn't imagine that.

The alleged killer could not imagine how the city of Charleston, under the good and wise leadership of Mayor Riley -- how the state of South Carolina, how the United States of America would respond -- not merely with revulsion at his evil act, but with big-hearted generosity and, more importantly, with a thoughtful introspection and self-examination that we so rarely see in public life.

Blinded by hatred, he failed to comprehend what Reverend Pinckney so well understood -- the power of God's grace.

This whole week, I've been reflecting on this idea of grace. The grace of the families who lost loved ones. The grace that Reverend Pinckney would preach about in his sermons. The grace described in one of my favorite hymnals -- the one we all know: Amazing grace, how sweet the sound that saved a wretch like me. I once was lost, but now I'm found; was blind but now I see.

According to the Christian tradition, grace is not earned. Grace is not merited. It's not something we deserve. Rather, grace is the free and benevolent favor of God -- as manifested in the salvation of sinners and the bestowal of blessings. Grace.

As a nation, out of this terrible tragedy, God has visited grace upon us, for he has allowed us to see where we've been blind. He has given us the chance, where we've been lost, to find our best selves. We may not have earned it, this grace, with our rancor and complacency, and short-sightedness and fear of each other -- but we got it all the same. He gave it to us anyway. He's once more given us grace. But it is up to us now to make the most of it, to receive it with gratitude, and to prove ourselves worthy of this gift.

For too long, we were blind to the pain that the Confederate flag stirred in too many of our citizens. It's true, a flag did not cause these murders. But as people from all walks of life, Republicans and Democrats, now acknowledge -- including Governor Haley, whose recent eloquence on the subject is worthy of praise -- as we all have to acknowledge, the flag has always represented more than just ancestral pride. For many, black and white, that flag was a reminder of systemic oppression and racial subjugation. We see that now.

Removing the flag from this state's capitol would not be an act of political correctness; it would not be an insult to the valor of Confederate soldiers. It would simply be an acknowledgment that the cause for which they fought -- the cause of slavery -- was wrong -- the imposition of Jim Crow after the Civil War, the resistance to civil rights for all people was wrong. It would be one step in an honest accounting of America's history; a modest but meaningful balm for so many unhealed wounds. It would be an expression of the amazing changes that have transformed this state and this country for the better, because of the work of so many people of goodwill, people of all races striving to form a more perfect union. By taking down that flag, we express God's grace.

But I don't think God wants us to stop there. For too long, we've been blind to the way past injustices continue to shape the present. Perhaps we see that now. Perhaps this tragedy causes us to ask some tough questions about how we can permit so many of our children to languish in poverty, or attend dilapidated schools, or grow up without prospects for a job or for a career.

Perhaps it causes us to examine what we're doing to cause some of our children to hate. Perhaps it softens hearts towards those lost young men, tens and tens of thousands caught up in the criminal justice system -- and leads us to make sure that that system is not infected with bias; that we embrace changes in how we train and equip our police so that the bonds of trust between law enforcement and the communities they serve make us all safer and more secure.

Maybe we now realize the way racial bias can infect us even when we don't realize it, so that we're guarding against not just racial slurs, but we're also guarding against the subtle impulse to call Johnny back for a job interview but not Jamal. So that we search our hearts when we consider laws to make it harder for some of our fellow citizens to vote. By recognizing our common humanity by treating every child as important, regardless of the color of their skin or the station into which they were born, and to do what's necessary to make opportunity real for every American -- by doing that, we express God's grace.

For too long --

AUDIENCE: For too long!

For too long, we've been blind to the unique mayhem that gun violence inflicts upon this nation. Sporadically, our eyes are open: When eight of our brothers and sisters are cut down in a church basement, 12 in a movie theater, 26 in an elementary school. But I hope we also see the 30 precious lives cut short by gun violence in this country every single day; the countless more whose lives are forever changed -- the survivors crippled, the children traumatized and fearful every day as they walk to school, the husband who will never feel his wife's warm touch, the entire communities whose grief overflows every time they have to watch what happened to them happen to some other place.

The vast majority of Americans -- the majority of gun owners -- want to do something about this. We see that now. And I'm convinced that by acknowledging the pain and loss of others, even as we respect the traditions and ways of life that make up this beloved country -- by making the moral choice to change, we express God's grace.

We don't earn grace. We're all sinners. We don't deserve it. But God gives it to us anyway. And we choose how to receive it. It's our decision how to honor it.

None of us can or should expect a transformation in race relations overnight. Every time something like this happens, somebody says we have to have a conversation about race. We talk a lot about race. There's no shortcut. And we don't need more talk. None of us should believe that a handful of gun safety measures will prevent every tragedy. It will not. People of goodwill will continue to debate the merits of various policies, as our democracy requires -- this is a big, raucous place, America is. And there are good people on both sides of these debates. Whatever solutions we find will necessarily be incomplete.

But it would be a betrayal of everything Reverend Pinckney stood for, I believe, if we allowed ourselves to slip into a comfortable silence again. Once the eulogies have been delivered, once the TV cameras move on, to go back to business as usual -- that's what we so often do to avoid uncomfortable truths about the prejudice that still infects our society. To settle for symbolic gestures without following up with the hard work of more lasting change -- that's how we lose our way again.

It would be a refutation of the forgiveness expressed by those families if we merely slipped into old habits, whereby those who disagree with us are not merely wrong but bad; where we shout instead of listen; where we barricade ourselves behind preconceived notions or well-practiced cynicism.

Reverend Pinckney once said, "Across the South, we have a deep appreciation of history -- we haven't always had a deep appreciation of each other's history." What is true in the South is true for America. Clem understood that justice grows out of recognition of ourselves in each other. That my liberty depends on you being free, too. That history can't be a sword to justify injustice, or a shield against progress, but must be a manual for how to avoid repeating the mistakes of the past -- how to break the cycle. A roadway toward a better world. He knew that the path of grace involves an open mind -- but, more importantly, an open heart.

That's what I've felt this week -- an open heart. That, more than any particular policy or analysis, is what's called upon right now, I think -- what a friend of mine, the writer Marilyn Robinson, calls "that reservoir of goodness, beyond, and of another kind, that we are able to do each other in the ordinary cause of things."

That reservoir of goodness. If we can find that grace, anything is possible. If we can tap that grace, everything can change.

Amazing grace. Amazing grace.

(Begins to sing) -- Amazing grace -- how sweet the sound, that saved a wretch like me; I once was lost, but now I'm found; was blind but now I see.

Clementa Pinckney found that grace.
Cynthia Hurd found that grace.
Susie Jackson found that grace.
Ethel Lance found that grace.
DePayne Middleton-Doctor found that grace.
Tywanza Sanders found that grace.
Daniel L. Simmons, Sr. found that grace.
Sharonda Coleman-Singleton found that grace.
Myra Thompson found that grace.

Through the example of their lives, they've now passed it on to us. May we find ourselves worthy of that precious and extraordinary gift, as long as our lives endure. May grace now lead them home. May God continue to shed His grace on the United States of America.

9 "We are born of immigrants."

Naturalization Ceremony at the National Archives
December 15, 2015
National Archives, Washington, D.C.

Well, good morning, everybody. Thank you Deputy
Secretary Mayorkas, Judge Roberts, and Director
Rodriguez. Thank you to our Archivist, David
Ferriero, and everyone at the National Archives for
hosting us here today in this spectacular setting.

And to my fellow Americans, our newest citizens --
I'm so excited. You are men and women from more
than 25 countries, from Brazil to Uganda, from Iraq
to the Philippines. You may come from teeming
cities or rural villages. You don't look alike. You
don't worship the same way. But here, surrounded
by the very documents whose values bind us together
as one people, you've raised your hand and sworn a
sacred oath. I'm proud to be among the first to greet
you as "my fellow Americans."

What a remarkable journey all of you have made.

And as of today, your story is forever woven into the larger story of this nation. In the brief time that we have together, I want to share that story with you. Because even as you've put in the work required to become a citizen, you still have a demanding and rewarding task ahead of you -- and that is the hard work of active citizenship. You have rights and you have responsibilities. And now you have to help us write the next great chapter in America's story.

Just about every nation in the world, to some extent, admits immigrants. But there's something unique about America. We don't simply welcome new immigrants, we don't simply welcome new arrivals -- we are born of immigrants. That is who we are. Immigration is our origin story. And for more than two centuries, it's remained at the core of our national character; it's our oldest tradition. It's who we are. It's part of what makes us exceptional.

After all, unless your family is Native American, one of the first Americans, our families -- all of our families -- come from someplace else. The first refugees were the Pilgrims themselves -- fleeing religious persecution, crossing the stormy Atlantic to reach a new world where they might live and pray freely. Eight signers of the Declaration of Independence were immigrants. And in those first decades after independence, English, German, and Scottish immigrants came over, huddled on creaky ships, seeking what Thomas Paine called "asylum for the persecuted lovers of civil and religious liberty..."

Down through the decades, Irish Catholics fleeing hunger, Italians fleeing poverty filled up our cities, rolled up their sleeves, built America. Chinese laborers jammed in steerage under the decks of steamships, making their way to California to build the Central Pacific Railroad that would transform the West -- and our nation. Wave after wave of men, women, and children -- from the Middle East and the Mediterranean, from Asia and Africa -- poured into Ellis Island, or Angel Island, their trunks bursting with their most cherished possessions -- maybe a photograph of the family they left behind, a family Bible, or a Torah, or a Koran. A bag in one hand, maybe a child in the other, standing for hours in long lines. New York and cities across America were transformed into a sort of global fashion show. You had Dutch lace caps and the North African fezzes, stodgy tweed suits and colorful Caribbean dresses.

And perhaps, like some of you, these new arrivals might have had some moments of doubt, wondering if they had made a mistake in leaving everything and everyone they ever knew behind. So life in America was not always easy. It wasn't always easy for new immigrants. Certainly it wasn't easy for those of African heritage who had not come here voluntarily, and yet in their own way were immigrants themselves. There was discrimination and hardship and poverty. But, like you, they no doubt found inspiration in all those who had come before them. And they were able to muster faith that, here in America, they might build a better life and give their children something more.

Just as so many have come here in search of a dream, others sought shelter from nightmares. Survivors of the Holocaust. Soviet Refuseniks. Refugees from Vietnam, Laos, Cambodia. Iraqis and Afghans fleeing war. Mexicans, Cubans, Iranians leaving behind deadly revolutions. Central American teenagers running from gang violence. The Lost Boys of Sudan escaping civil war. They're people like Fulbert Florent Akoula from the Republic of Congo, who was granted asylum when his family was threatened by political violence. And today, Fulbert is here, a proud American.

We can never say it often or loudly enough: Immigrants and refugees revitalize and renew America. Immigrants like you are more likely to start your own business. Many of the Fortune 500 companies in this country were founded by immigrants or their children. Many of the tech startups in Silicon Valley have at least one immigrant founder.

Immigrants are the teachers who inspire our children, and they're the doctors who keep us healthy. They're the engineers who design our skylines, and the artists and the entertainers who touch our hearts. Immigrants are soldiers, sailors, airmen, Marines, Coast Guardsmen who protect us, often risking their lives for an America that isn't even their own yet. As an Iraqi, Muhanned Ibrahim Al Naib was the target of death threats for working with American forces. He stood by his American comrades, and came to the U.S. as a refugee. And today, we stand by him. And we are proud to welcome Muhanned as a citizen of the country that he already helped to defend.

We celebrate this history, this heritage, as an immigrant nation. And we are strong enough to acknowledge, as painful as it may be, that we haven't always lived up to our own ideals. We haven't always lived up to these documents.

From the start, Africans were brought here in chains against their will, and then toiled under the whip. They also built America. A century ago, New York City shops displayed those signs, "No Irish Need Apply." Catholics were targeted, their loyalty questioned -- so much so that as recently as the 1950s and '60s, when JFK had to run, he had to convince people that his allegiance wasn't primarily to the Pope.

Chinese immigrants faced persecution and vicious stereotypes, and were, for a time, even banned from entering America. During World War II, German and Italian residents were detained, and in one of the darkest chapters in our history, Japanese immigrants and even Japanese American citizens were forced from their homes and imprisoned in camps. We succumbed to fear. We betrayed not only our fellow Americans, but our deepest values. We betrayed these documents. It's happened before.

And the biggest irony of course was -- is that those who betrayed these values were themselves the children of immigrants. How quickly we forget. One generation passes, two generation passes, and suddenly we don't remember where we came from. And we suggest that somehow there is "us" and there is "them," not remembering we used to be "them."

On days like today, we need to resolve never to repeat mistakes like that again.

We must resolve to always speak out against hatred and bigotry in all of its forms -- whether taunts against the child of an immigrant farmworker or threats against a Muslim shopkeeper. We are Americans. Standing up for each other is what the values enshrined in the documents in this room compels us to do -- especially when it's hard. Especially when it's not convenient. That's when it counts. That's when it matters -- not when things are easy, but when things are hard.

The truth is, being an American is hard. Being part of a democratic government is hard. Being a citizen is hard. It is a challenge. It's supposed to be. There's no respite from our ideals. All of us are called to live up to our expectations for ourselves -- not just when it's convenient, but when it's inconvenient. When it's tough. When we're afraid. The tension throughout our history between welcoming or rejecting the stranger, it's about more than just immigration. It's about the meaning of America, what kind of country do we want to be. It's about the capacity of each generation to honor the creed as old as our founding: "E Pluribus Unum" -- that out of many, we are one.

Scripture tells us, "For we are strangers before you, and sojourners, as were all our fathers." "We are strangers before you." In the Mexican immigrant today, we see the Catholic immigrant of a century ago. In the Syrian seeking refuge today, we should see the Jewish refugee of World War II. In these new Americans, we see our own American stories -- our parents, our grandparents, our aunts, our uncles, our cousins who packed up what they could and scraped together what they had. And their paperwork wasn't always in order. And they set out for a place that was more than just a piece of land, but an idea.

America: A place where we can be a part of something bigger. A place where we can contribute our talents and fulfill our ambitions and secure new opportunity for ourselves and for others. A place where we can retain pride in our heritage, but where we recognize that we have a common creed, a loyalty to these documents, a loyalty to our democracy; where we can criticize our government, but understand that we love it; where we agree to live together even when we don't agree with each other; where we work through the democratic process, and not through violence or sectarianism to resolve disputes; where we live side by side as neighbors; and where our children know themselves to be a part of this nation, no longer strangers, but the bedrock of this nation, the essence of this nation.

And that's why today is not the final step in your journey. More than 60 years ago, at a ceremony like this one, Senator John F. Kennedy said, "No form of government requires more of its citizens than does the American democracy." Our system of self-government depends on ordinary citizens doing the hard, frustrating but always essential work of citizenship -- of being informed. Of understanding that the government isn't some distant thing, but is you. Of speaking out when something is not right.

Of helping fellow citizens when they need a hand. Of coming together to shape our country's course.

And that work gives purpose to every generation. It belongs to me. It belongs to the judge. It belongs to you. It belongs to you, all of us, as citizens. To follow our laws, yes, but also to engage with your communities and to speak up for what you believe in. And to vote -- to not only exercise the rights that are now yours, but to stand up for the rights of others.

Birtukan Gudeya is here from Ethiopia. She said, "The joy of being an American is the joy of freedom and opportunity. We have been handed a work in progress, one that can evolve for the good of all Americans." I couldn't have said it better.

That is what makes America great -- not just the words on these founding documents, as precious and valuable as they are, but the progress that they've inspired. If you ever wonder whether America is big enough to hold multitudes, strong enough to withstand the forces of change, brave enough to live up to our ideals even in times of trial, then look to the generations of ordinary citizens who have proven again and again that we are worthy of that.

That's our great inheritance -- what ordinary people have done to build this country and make these words live. And it's our generation's task to follow their example in this journey -- to keep building an America where no matter who we are or what we look like, or who we love or what we believe, we can make of our lives what we will.

You will not and should not forget your history and your past. That adds to the richness of American life. But you are now American. You've got obligations as citizens. And I'm absolutely confident you will meet them. You'll set a good example for all of us, because you know how precious this thing is. It's not something to take for granted. It's something to cherish and to fight for.

Thank you. May god bless you. May god bless the United States of America.

10 "We force ourselves to feel the dread of children confused by what they see."

Hiroshima Peace Memorial
May 27, 2016
Hiroshima Peace Park, Hiroshima, Japan

On May 27, 2016 Obama became the first sitting US President to visit Hiroshima, bombed by the US in 1945. Delivered at the Hiroshima Peace Park to a small audience of around 100 people, including hibakusha (atomic bomb survivors).

Seventy-one years ago, on a bright, cloudless morning, death fell from the sky and the world was changed. A flash of light and a wall of fire destroyed a city and demonstrated that mankind possessed the means to destroy itself.

Why do we come to this place, to Hiroshima? We come to ponder a terrible force unleashed in a not so distant past. We come to mourn the dead, including over 100,000 in Japanese men, women and children; thousands of Koreans; a dozen Americans held prisoner. Their souls speak to us. They ask us to look inward, to take stock of who we are and what we might become.

It is not the fact of war that sets Hiroshima apart. Artifacts tell us that violent conflict appeared with the very first man. Our early ancestors, having learned to make blades from flint and spears from wood, used these tools not just for hunting, but against their own kind. On every continent, the history of civilization is filled with war, whether driven by scarcity of grain or hunger for gold; compelled by nationalist fervor or religious zeal. Empires have risen and fallen. Peoples have been subjugated and liberated. And at each juncture, innocents have suffered, a countless toll, their names forgotten by time.

The World War that reached its brutal end in Hiroshima and Nagasaki was fought among the wealthiest and most powerful of nations. Their civilizations had given the world great cities and magnificent art. Their thinkers had advanced ideas of justice and harmony and truth. And yet, the war grew out of the same base instinct for domination or conquest that had caused conflicts among the simplest tribes; an old pattern amplified by new capabilities and without new constraints. In the span of a few years, some 60 million people would die -- men, women, children no different than us, shot, beaten, marched, bombed, jailed, starved, gassed to death.

There are many sites around the world that chronicle this war -- memorials that tell stories of courage and heroism; graves and empty camps that echo of unspeakable depravity. Yet in the image of a mushroom cloud that rose into these skies, we are most starkly reminded of humanity's core contradiction; how the very spark that marks us as a species -- our thoughts, our imagination, our language, our tool-making, our ability to set ourselves apart from nature and bend it to our will -- those very things also give us the capacity for unmatched destruction.

How often does material advancement or social innovation blind us to this truth. How easily we learn to justify violence in the name of some higher cause. Every great religion promises a pathway to love and peace and righteousness, and yet no religion has been spared from believers who have claimed their faith as a license to kill. Nations arise, telling a story that binds people together in sacrifice and cooperation, allowing for remarkable feats, but those same stories have so often been used to oppress and dehumanize those who are different.

Science allows us to communicate across the seas and fly above the clouds; to cure disease and understand the cosmos. But those same discoveries can be turned into ever-more efficient killing machines.

The wars of the modern age teach this truth. Hiroshima teaches this truth. Technological progress without an equivalent progress in human institutions can doom us. The scientific revolution that led to the splitting of an atom requires a moral revolution, as well.

That is why we come to this place. We stand here, in the middle of this city, and force ourselves to imagine the moment the bomb fell. We force ourselves to feel the dread of children confused by what they see. We listen to a silent cry. We remember all the innocents killed across the arc of that terrible war, and the wars that came before, and the wars that would follow.

Mere words cannot give voice to such suffering, but we have a shared responsibility to look directly into the eye of history and ask what we must do differently to curb such suffering again. Someday the voices of the hibakusha will no longer be with us to bear witness. But the memory of the morning of August 6th, 1945 must never fade. That memory allows us to fight complacency. It fuels our moral imagination. It allows us to change.

And since that fateful day, we have made choices that give us hope. The United States and Japan forged not only an alliance, but a friendship that has won far more for our people than we could ever claim through war. The nations of Europe built a Union that replaced battlefields with bonds of commerce and democracy. Oppressed peoples and nations won liberation. An international community established institutions and treaties that worked to avoid war and aspire to restrict and roll back, and ultimately eliminate the existence of nuclear weapons.

Still, every act of aggression between nations; every act of terror and corruption and cruelty and oppression that we see around the world shows our work is never done. We may not be able to eliminate man's capacity to do evil, so nations -- and the alliances that we've formed -- must possess the means to defend ourselves. But among those nations like my own that hold nuclear stockpiles, we must have the courage to escape the logic of fear, and pursue a world without them.

We may not realize this goal in my lifetime. But persistent effort can roll back the possibility of catastrophe. We can chart a course that leads to the destruction of these stockpiles. We can stop the spread to new nations, and secure deadly materials from fanatics.

And yet that is not enough. For we see around the world today how even the crudest rifles and barrel bombs can serve up violence on a terrible scale. We must change our mindset about war itself -- to prevent conflict through diplomacy, and strive to end conflicts after they've begun; to see our growing interdependence as a cause for peaceful cooperation and not violent competition; to define our nations not by our capacity to destroy, but by what we build.

And perhaps above all, we must reimagine our connection to one another as members of one human race. For this, too, is what makes our species unique. We're not bound by genetic code to repeat the mistakes of the past. We can learn. We can choose. We can tell our children a different story -- one that describes a common humanity; one that makes war less likely and cruelty less easily accepted.

We see these stories in the hibakusha -- the woman

who forgave a pilot who flew the plane that dropped the atomic bomb, because she recognized that what she really hated was war itself; the man who sought out families of Americans killed here, because he believed their loss was equal to his own.

My own nation's story began with simple words: All men are created equal, and endowed by our Creator with certain unalienable rights, including life, liberty and the pursuit of happiness. Realizing that ideal has never been easy, even within our own borders, even among our own citizens.

But staying true to that story is worth the effort. It is an ideal to be strived for; an ideal that extends across continents, and across oceans. The irreducible worth of every person, the insistence that every life is precious; the radical and necessary notion that we are part of a single human family -- that is the story that we all must tell.

That is why we come to Hiroshima. So that we might think of people we love -- the first smile from our children in the morning; the gentle touch from a spouse over the kitchen table; the comforting embrace of a parent -- we can think of those things and know that those same precious moments took place here seventy-one years ago. Those who died -- they are like us. Ordinary people understand this, I think. They do not want more war. They would rather that the wonders of science be focused on improving life, and not eliminating it.

When the choices made by nations, when the choices made by leaders reflect this simple wisdom, then the lesson of Hiroshima is done.

The world was forever changed here. But today, the children of this city will go through their day in peace. What a precious thing that is. It is worth protecting, and then extending to every child. That is the future we can choose -- a future in which Hiroshima and Nagasaki are known not as the dawn of atomic warfare, but as the start of our own moral awakening.

11 "Everyone here is someone's hero."

Memorial Day at Arlington Cemetery
May 30, 2016
Arlington Cemetery, Arlington, Virginia

President Barack Obama pays tribute to U.S. military personnel and their families in his final Memorial Day speech as Commander-in-Chief at Arlington National Cemetery.

I'm honored to be with you once again as we pay our respects, as Americans, to those who gave their lives for us all.

Here, at Arlington, the deafening sounds of combat have given way to the silence of these sacred hills. The chaos and confusion of battle has yielded to perfect, precise rows of peace. The Americans who rest here, and their families -- the best of us, those from whom we asked everything -- ask of us today only one thing in return: that we remember them.

If you look closely at the white markers that grace these hills, one thing you'll notice is that so many of the years -- dates of birth and dates of death -- are so close together. They belong to young Americans; those who never lived to be honored as veterans for their service -- men who battled their own brothers in Civil War, those who fought as a band of brothers an ocean away, men and women who redefine heroism for a new generation.

There are generals buried beside privates they led. Americans known as "Dad" or "Mom." Some only known to God. As Mr. Hallinan, a Marine who then watched over these grounds has said, "everyone here is someone's hero."

Those who rest beneath this silence -- not only here at Arlington, but at veterans' cemeteries across our country and around the world, and all who still remain missing -- they didn't speak the loudest about their patriotism. They let their actions do that. Whether they stood up in times of war, signed up in times of peace, or were called up by a draft board, they embodied the best of America.

As Commander-in-Chief, I have no greater responsibility than leading our men and women in uniform; I have no more solemn obligation sending them into harm's way. I think about this every time I approve an operation as President. Every time, as a husband and father, that I sign a condolence letter. Every time Michelle and I sit at the bedside of a wounded warrior or grieve and hug members of a

Gold Star Family.

Less than one percent of our nation wears the uniform, and so few Americans sees this patriotism with their own eyes or knows someone who exemplifies it. But every day, there are American families who pray for the sound of a familiar voice when the phone rings. For the sound of a loved one's letter or email arriving. More than one million times in our history, it didn't come. And instead, a car pulled up to the house. And there was a knock on the front door. And the sounds of Taps floated through a cemetery's trees.

For us, the living -- those of us who still have a voice -- it is our responsibility, our obligation, to fill that silence with our love and our support and our gratitude -- and not just with our words, but with our actions. For truly remembering, and truly honoring these fallen Americans means being there for their parents, and their spouses, and their children -- like the boys and girls here today, wearing red shirts and bearing photos of the fallen. Your moms and dads would be so proud of you. And we are, too.

Truly remembering means that after our fallen heroes gave everything to get their battle buddies home, we have to make sure our veterans get everything that they have earned, from good health care to a good job. And we have to do better; our work is never done. We have to be there not only when we need them, but when they need us.

Thirty days before he would be laid to rest a short

walk from here, President Kennedy told us that a nation reveals itself not only by the people it produces, but by those it remembers. Not everyone will serve. Not everyone will visit this national sanctuary. But we remember our best in every corner of our country from which they came. We remember them by teaching our children at schools with fallen heroes' names, like Dorie Miller Elementary in San Antonio. Or being good neighbors in communities named after great generals, like McPherson, Kansas. Or when we walk down 1st Sgt. Bobby Mendez Way in Brooklyn, or drive across the Hoover Dam on a bridge that bears Pat Tillman's name.

We reveal ourselves in our words and deeds, but also by the simple act of listening. My fellow Americans, today and every day, listen to the stories these Gold Star families and veterans have to tell. Ask about who he or she was, why they volunteered. Hear from those who loved them about what their smile looked like, and their laugh sounded like, and the dreams they had for their lives.

Since we gathered here one year ago, more than 20 brave Americans have given their lives for the security of our people in Afghanistan. We pray for them all, and for their families. In Iraq, in our fight against ISIL, three Americans have given their lives in combat on our behalf. And today, I ask you to remember their stories, as well.

Charles Keating, IV -- Charlie, or Chuck, or "C-4" -- was born into a family of veterans, All-American athletes and Olympians -- even a Gold Medalist. So, naturally, Charlie, and the love of his life, Brooke, celebrated their anniversary on the Fourth of July. She called him the "huge goofball" everybody wanted to be friends with -- the adventurer who surfed and spearfished and planned to sail around the world.

When the Twin Towers fell, he was in high school, and he decided to enlist -- joined the SEALs because, he told his friends, it was the hardest thing to do. He deployed to Afghanistan and three times to Iraq, earning a Bronze Star for valor. Earlier this month, while assisting local forces in Iraq who had come under attack, he gave his life.

A few days later, one of his platoon mates sent Charlie's parents a letter from Iraq. "Please tell everyone Chuck saved a lot of lives today," it said. He left us, "with that big signature smile on his handsome face, as always. Chuck was full of aloha, but was also a ferocious warrior." Today, we honor Chief Special Warfare Officer Charles Keating IV.

Louis Cardin was the sixth of seven children, a Californian with an infectious wit who always had a joke at the ready to help someone get through a tough time. When his siblings ran around the house as kids, his mom, Pat, would yell after them: "Watch that baby's safety margin!" Today, she realizes that what she was really doing was raising a Marine. As a teenager, he proudly signed up. Louie graduated high school on a Friday. Three days later, on Monday morning, the Marines came to pick him up. That was 10 years ago. One morning this March, a Marine knocked on his mother's door again. On his fifth tour, at a fire base in Iraq, Louie gave his life while protecting the Marines under his command.

Putting others before himself was what Louie did best. He chose to live in the barracks with his buddies even when he could have taken a house off base. He volunteered to babysit for friends who needed a date night. He'd just earned a promotion to mentor his fellow Marines. When they brought Louie home, hundreds of strangers lined freeway overpasses and the streets of Southern California to salute him. And today, we salute Staff Sergeant Louis Cardin.

Joshua Wheeler's sister says he was "exactly what was right about this world. He came from nothing and he really made something of himself." As a kid, Josh was the one who made sure his brother and four half-sisters were dressed and fed and off to school. When there wasn't food in the cupboard, he grabbed his hunting rifle and came back with a deer for dinner. When his country needed him, he enlisted in the Army at age 19.

He deployed to Iraq and Afghanistan -- 14 times; earned 11 Bronze Stars, four for valor. Last October, as ISIL terrorists prepared to execute 70 hostages, Josh and his fellow Special Ops went in and rescued them. Every single one walked free. "We were already dead," one of the hostages said, "then God sent us a force from the sky." That force was the U.S. Army, including Josh Wheeler.

Josh was the doting dad who wrote notes to his kids in the stacks of books he read. Flying home last summer to be with his wife, Ashley, who was about to give birth, he scribbled one note in the novel he was reading, just to tell his unborn son he was on his way. Ashley Wheeler is with us here today, holding their 10-month-old son, David. Ashley says Josh's memory makes her think about how can she be a better citizen. And she hopes it's what other people think about, too. Today, this husband and father rests here, in Arlington, in Section 60. And as Americans, we resolve to be better -- better people, better citizens, because of Master Sergeant Joshua Wheeler.

A nation reveals itself not only by the people it produces, but by those it remembers. We do so not just by hoisting a flag, but by lifting up our neighbors. Not just by pausing in silence, but by practicing in our own lives the ideals of opportunity and liberty and equality that they fought for. We can serve others, and contribute to the causes they believed in, and above all, keep their stories alive so that one day, when he grows up and thinks of his dad, an American like David Wheeler can tell them, as well, the stories of the lives that others gave for all of us.

We are so proud of them. We are so grateful for their sacrifice. We are so thankful to those families of the fallen. May God bless our fallen and their families. May He bless all of you. And may He forever bless these United States of America.

12 "A stone worn down by the tragedy of over a thousand bare feet."

Dedication of the National Museum of African American History and Culture
September 24, 2016
National Mall, Washington, D.C.

James Baldwin once wrote, "For while the tale of how we suffer, and how we are delighted, and how we may triumph is never new, it always must be heard." For while the tale of how we suffer, and how we are delighted, and how we may triumph is never new, it always must be heard.

Today, as so many generations have before, we gather on our National Mall to tell an essential part of our American story -- one that has at times been overlooked -- we come not just for today, but for all time.

President and Mrs. Bush; President Clinton; Vice President and Dr. Biden; Chief Justice Roberts; Secretary Skorton; Reverend Butts; distinguished guests: Thank you. Thank you for your leadership in making sure this tale is told. We're here in part because of you and because of all those Americans -- the Civil War vets, the Civil Rights foot soldiers, the champions of this effort on Capitol Hill -- who, for more than a century, kept the dream of this museum alive.

That includes our leaders in Congress -- Paul Ryan and Nancy Pelosi. It includes one of my heroes, John Lewis, who, as he has so often, took the torch from those who came before him and brought us past the finish line. It includes the philanthropists and benefactors and advisory members who have so generously given not only their money but their time. It includes the Americans who offered up all the family keepsakes tucked away in Grandma's attic. And of course, it includes a man without whose vision and passion and persistence we would not be here today -- Mr. Lonnie Bunch.

What we can see of this building -- the towering glass, the artistry of the metalwork -- is surely a sight to behold. But beyond the majesty of the building, what makes this occasion so special is the larger story it contains. Below us, this building reaches down 70 feet, its roots spreading far wider and deeper than any tree on this Mall. And on its lowest level, after you walk past remnants of a slave ship, after you reflect on the immortal declaration that "all men are created equal," you can see a block of stone. On top of this stone sits a historical marker, weathered by the ages. That marker reads: "General Andrew Jackson and Henry Clay spoke from this slave block...during the year 1830."

I want you to think about this. Consider what this artifact tells us about history, about how it's told, and about what can be cast aside. On a stone where day after day, for years, men and women were torn from their spouse or their child, shackled and bound, and bought and sold, and bid like cattle; on a stone worn down by the tragedy of over a thousand bare feet -- for a long time, the only thing we considered important, the singular thing we once chose to commemorate as "history" with a plaque were the unmemorable speeches of two powerful men.

And that block I think explains why this museum is so necessary. Because that same object, reframed, put in context, tells us so much more. As Americans, we rightfully passed on the tales of the giants who built this country; who led armies into battle and waged seminal debates in the halls of Congress and the corridors of power. But too often, we ignored or forgot the stories of millions upon millions of others, who built this nation just as surely, whose humble eloquence, whose calloused hands, whose steady drive helped to create cities, erect industries, build the arsenals of democracy.

And so this national museum helps to tell a richer and fuller story of who we are. It helps us better understand the lives, yes, of the President, but also the slave; the industrialist, but also the porter; the keeper of the status quo, but also of the activist seeking to overthrow that status quo; the teacher or the cook, alongside the statesman. And by knowing this other story, we better understand ourselves and each other. It binds us together. It reaffirms that all of us are America -- that African-American history is not somehow separate from our larger American story, it's not the underside of the American story, it is central to the American story. That our glory derives not just from our most obvious triumphs, but how we've wrested triumph from tragedy, and how we've been able to remake ourselves, again and again and again, in accordance with our highest ideals.

I, too, am America.

The great historian John Hope Franklin, who helped to get this museum started, once said, "Good history is a good foundation for a better present and future." He understood the best history doesn't just sit behind a glass case; it helps us to understand what's outside the case. The best history helps us recognize the mistakes that we've made and the dark corners of the human spirit that we need to guard against. And, yes, a clear-eyed view of history can make us uncomfortable, and shake us out of familiar narratives. But it is precisely because of that discomfort that we learn and grow and harness our collective power to make this nation more perfect.

That's the American story that this museum tells -- one of suffering and delight; one of fear but also of hope; of wandering in the wilderness and then seeing out on the horizon a glimmer of the Promised Land.

It is in this embrace of truth, as best as we can know it, in the celebration of the entire American experience, where real patriotism lies. As President Bush just said, a great nation doesn't shy from the truth. It strengthens us. It emboldens us. It should fortify us. It is an act of patriotism to understand where we've been. And this museum tells the story of so many patriots.

Yes, African Americans have felt the cold weight of shackles and the stinging lash of the field whip. But we've also dared to run north, and sing songs from Harriet Tubman's hymnal. We've buttoned up our Union Blues to join the fight for our freedom. We've railed against injustice for decade upon decade -- a lifetime of struggle, and progress, and enlightenment that we see etched in Frederick Douglass's mighty, leonine gaze.

Yes, this museum tells a story of people who felt the indignity, the small and large humiliations of a "whites only" sign, or wept at the side of Emmett Till's coffin, or fell to their knees on shards of stained glass outside a church where four little girls died. But it also tells the story of the black youth and white youth sitting alongside each other, straight-backed, so full of dignity on those lunch counter stools; the story of a six-year-old Ruby Bridges, pigtails, fresh-pressed dress, walking that gauntlet to get to school; Tuskegee airmen soaring the skies not just to beat a dictator, but to reaffirm the promise of our democracy -- but remind us that all of us are created equal.

This is the place to understand how protest and love of country don't merely coexist but inform each other; how men can proudly win the gold for their country but still insist on raising a black-gloved fist; how we can wear "I Can't Breathe"

T-shirt and still grieve for fallen police officers. Here's the America where the razor-sharp uniform of the Chairman of the Joint Chiefs of Staff belongs alongside the cape of the Godfather of Soul. We have shown the world that we can float like butterflies and sting like bees; that we can rocket into space like Mae Jemison, steal home like Jackie, rock like Jimi, stir the pot like Richard Pryor; or we can be sick and tired of being sick and tired, like Fannie Lou Hamer, and still Rock Steady like Aretha Franklin.

We are large, Walt Whitman told us, containing multitudes. We are large, containing multitudes. Full of contradictions. That's America. That's what makes us grow. That's what makes us extraordinary. And as is true for America, so is true for African American experience. We're not a burden on America, or a stain on America, or an object of pity or charity for America. We're America.

And that's what this museum explains -- the fact that our stories have shaped every corner of our culture. The struggles for freedom that took place made our Constitution a real and living document, tested and shaped and deepened and made more profound its meaning for all people. The story told here doesn't just belong to black Americans; it belongs to all Americans -- for the African-American experience has been shaped just as much by Europeans and Asians and Native Americans and Latinos. We have informed each other. We are polyglot, a stew.

Scripture promised that if we lift up the oppressed, then our light will rise in the darkness, and our night will become like the noonday. And the story contained in this museum makes those words prophecy. And that's what this day is about. That's what this museum is about. I, too, am America. It is a glorious story, the one that's told here. It is complicated and it is messy and it is full of contradictions, as all great stories are, as Shakespeare is, as Scripture is. And it's a story that perhaps needs to be told now more than ever.

A museum alone will not alleviate poverty in every inner city or every rural hamlet. It won't eliminate gun violence from all our neighborhoods, or immediately ensure that justice is always colorblind. It won't wipe away every instance of discrimination in a job interview or a sentencing hearing or folks trying to rent an apartment. Those things are up to us, the decisions and choices we make. It requires speaking out, and organizing, and voting, until our values are fully reflected in our laws and our policies and our communities.

But what this museum does show us is that in even the face of oppression, even in the face of unimaginable difficulty, America has moved forward. And so this museum provides context for the debates of our times. It illuminates them and gives us some sense of how they evolved, and perhaps keeps them in proportion. Perhaps it can help a white visitor understand the pain and anger of demonstrators in places like Tulsa and Charlotte. But it can also help black visitors appreciate the fact that not only is this younger generation carrying on traditions of the past but, within the white communities across this nation we see the sincerity of law enforcement officers and officials who, in fits and starts, are struggling to understand, and are trying to do the right thing.

It reminds us that routine discrimination and Jim Crow aren't ancient history, it's just a blink in the eye of history. It was just yesterday. And so we should not be surprised that not all the healing is done. We shouldn't despair that it's not all solved. And knowing the larger story should instead remind us of just how remarkable the changes that have taken place truly are -- just in my lifetime -- and thereby inspire us to further progress.

And so hopefully this museum can help us talk to each other. And more importantly, listen to each other. And most importantly, see each other. Black and white and Latino and Native American and Asian American -- see how our stories are bound together. And bound together with women in America, and workers in America, and entrepreneurs in America, and LGBT Americans. And for young people who didn't live through the struggles represented here, I hope you draw strength from the changes that have taken place. Come here and see the power of your own agency. See how young John Lewis was. These were children who transformed a nation in a blink of an eye. Young people, come here and see your ability to make your mark.

The very fact of this day does not prove that America is perfect, but it does validate the ideas of our founding, that this country born of change, this country born of revolution, this country of we, the people, this country can get better.

And that's why we celebrate, mindful that our work is not yet done; mindful that we are but on a waystation on this common journey towards freedom. And how glorious it is that we enshrine it here, on some of our nation's most hallowed ground -- the same place where lives were once traded but also where hundreds of thousands of Americans, of all colors and creeds, once marched. How joyful it is that this story take its rightful place -- alongside Jefferson who declared our independence, and Washington who made it real, and alongside Lincoln who saved our union, and the GIs who defended it; alongside a new monument to a King, gazing outward, summoning us toward that mountaintop. How righteous it is that with tell this story here.

For almost eight years, I have been blessed with the extraordinary honor of serving you in this office. Time and again, I've flown low over this mall on Marine One, often with Michelle and our daughters. And President Clinton, President Bush, they'll tell you it is incredible sight. We pass right across the Washington Monument -- it feels like you can reach out and touch it. And at night, if you turn the other way, you don't just see the Lincoln Memorial, Old Abe is lit up and you can see him, his spirit glowing from that building. And we don't have many trips left. But over the years, I've always been comforted as I've watched this museum rise from this earth into this remarkable tribute. Because I know that years from now, like all of you, Michelle and I will be able to come here to this museum, and not just bring our kids but hopefully our grandkids. I imagine holding a little hand of somebody and tell them the stories that are enshrined here.

And in the years that follow, they'll be able to do the same. And then we'll go to the Lincoln Memorial and we'll take in the view atop the Washington Monument. And together, we'll learn about ourselves, as Americans -- our sufferings, our delights, and our triumphs. And we'll walk away better for it, better because the better grasp of history. We'll walk away that much more in love with this country, the only place on Earth where this story could have unfolded.

It is a monument, no less than the others on this Mall, to the deep and abiding love for this country, and the ideals upon which it is founded. For we, too, are America.

So enough talk. President Bush is timing me. He had the over/under at 25. Let us now open this museum to the world. Today, we have with us a family that reflects the arc of our progress: the Bonner family -- four generations in all, starting with gorgeous seven-year-old Christine and going up to gorgeous 99-year-old Ruth.

Now, Ruth's father, Elijah Odom, was born into servitude in Mississippi. He was born a slave. As a young boy, he ran, though, to his freedom. He lived through Reconstruction and he lived through Jim Crow. But he went on to farm, and graduate from medical school, and gave life to the beautiful family that we see today -- with a spirit reflected in beautiful Christine, free and equal in the laws of her country and in the eyes of God.

So in a brief moment, their family will join us in ringing a bell from the First Baptist Church in Virginia -- one of the oldest black churches in America, founded under a grove of trees in 1776. And the sound of this bell will be echoed by others in houses of worship and town squares all across this country -- an echo of the ringing bells that signaled Emancipation more than a century and a half ago; the sound, and the anthem, of American freedom.

God bless you all. God bless the United States of America.

13 "The end of the Republic has never looked better."

White House Correspondents' Association Dinner 2016
April 30, 2016
Capital Hilton, Washington, D.C.

(Entrance music: "When I'm Gone" by Anna Kendrick.)

You can't say it, but you know it's true. (Laughter.)

Good evening, everybody. It is an honor to be here at my last -- and perhaps the last -- White House Correspondents' Dinner. (Laughter and applause.)

You all look great. The end of the Republic has never looked better. (Laughter and applause.)

I do apologize -- I know I was a little late tonight. I was running on C.P.T. -- (laughter) -- which stands for "jokes that white people should not make."

(Laughter and applause.) It's a tip for you, Jeff. (Laughter.)

Anyway, here we are. My eighth and final appearance at this unique event. (Laughter.) And I am excited. If this material works well, I'm going to use it at Goldman Sachs next year. (Laughter and applause.) Earn me some serious Tubmans. That's right. (Laughter and applause.)

My brilliant and beautiful wife, Michelle, is here tonight. (Applause.) She looks so happy to be here. (Laughter.) That's called practice -- it's like learning to do three-minute planks. (Laughter.) She makes it look easy now. (Laughter.)

Next year at this time, someone else will be standing here in this very spot, and it's anyone's guess who she will be. (Laughter and applause.) But standing here, I can't help but be reflective, a little sentimental. Eight years ago, I said it was time to change the tone of our politics. In hindsight, I clearly should have been more specific. (Laughter.)

Eight years ago, I was a young man, full of idealism and vigor, and look at me now. (Laughter.) I am gray and grizzled, just counting down the days 'til my death panel. (Laughter and applause.) Hillary once questioned whether I'd be ready for a 3 a.m. phone call -- now I'm awake anyway because I've got to go to the bathroom. (Laughter and applause.) I'm up.

In fact, somebody recently said to me, Mr. President, you are so yesterday; Justin Trudeau has completely replaced you -- he's so handsome, he's so charming, he's the future. And I said, Justin, just give it a rest. (Laughter and applause.) I resented that. (Laughter.)

Meanwhile, Michelle has not aged a day. (Applause.) The only way you can date her in photos is by looking at me. (Laughter.) Take a look.
Here we are in 2008. (Slide is shown.)

Here we are a few years later. (Slide is shown.)

And this one is from two weeks ago. (Slide is shown of Michelle next to a skeleton.) (Laughter and applause.)

So time passes. (Laughter.) In just six short months, I will be officially a lame duck, which means Congress now will flat-out reject my authority. (Laughter.) And Republican leaders won't take my phone calls. And this is going to take some getting used to, it's really going to -- it's a curve ball. I don't know what to do with it. (Laughter.)

Of course, in fact, for months now congressional Republicans have been saying there are things I cannot do in my final year. Unfortunately, this dinner was not one of them. (Laughter.) But on everything else, it's another story. And you know who you are, Republicans. In fact, I think we've got Republican Senators Tim Scott and Cory Gardner, they're in the house, which reminds me, security, bar the doors! (Laughter.) Judge Merrick Garland, come on out, we're going to do this right here, right now. (Applause.) It's like "The Red Wedding." (Laughter.)

But it's not just Congress. Even some foreign leaders,

they've been looking ahead, anticipating my departure. Last week, Prince George showed up to our meeting in his bathrobe. (Laughter and applause.) That was a slap in the face. (Laughter.) A clear breach in protocol. (Laughter.) Although while in England I did have lunch with Her Majesty, the Queen, took in a performance of Shakespeare, hit the links with David Cameron -- just in case anybody is still debating whether I'm black enough, I think that settles the debate. (Laughter and applause.)

I won't lie -- look, this is a tough transition. It's hard. Key staff are now starting to leave the White House. Even reporters have left me. Savannah Guthrie, she's left the White House Press Corps to host the Today show. Norah O'Donnell left the briefing room to host CBS This Morning. Jake Tapper left journalism to join CNN. (Laughter and applause.)

But the prospect of leaving the White House is a mixed bag. You might have heard that someone jumped the White House fence last week, but I have to give Secret Service credit -- they found Michelle, brought her back, she's safe back at home now. (Laughter and applause.) It's only nine more months, baby. Settle down. (Laughter.)

And yet, somehow, despite all this, despite the churn, in my final year, my approval ratings keep going up. (Laughter.) The last time I was this high, I was trying to decide on my major. (Laughter and applause.)

And here's the thing: I haven't really done anything differently. So it's odd. Even my aides can't explain the rising poll numbers -- what has changed, nobody can figure it out. (Slide is shown.) (Laughter and applause.) Puzzling.

Anyway, in this last year I do have more appreciation for those who have been with me on this amazing ride, like one of our finest public servants, Joe Biden. God bless him. Love that guy. (Applause.) I love Joe Biden, I really do. And I want to thank him for his friendship, for his counsel, for always giving it to me straight, for not shooting anybody in the face. (Laughter.) Thank you, Joe. (Laughter.)

Also, I would be remiss -- let's give it up for our host, Larry Wilmore. (Applause.) Also known as one of the two black guys who is not Jon Stewart. (Laughter.) You're the South African guy, right? (Laughter.) I love Larry. And his parents are here, who are from Evanston, which is a great town. (Applause.)

I also would like to acknowledge some of the award-winning reporters that we have with us here tonight. Rachel McAdams. Mark Ruffalo. Liev Schreiber. (Laughter.) Thank you all for everything that you've done. (Laughter.) I'm just joking. As you know, "Spotlight" is a film, a movie about investigative journalists with the resources and the autonomy to chase down the truth and hold the powerful accountable. Best fantasy film since Star Wars. (Laughter.) Look -- that was maybe a cheap shot. (Laughter.)

I understand the news business is tough these days, it keeps changing all the time. Every year at this dinner, somebody makes a joke about BuzzFeed, for example, changing the media landscape. And every year, the Washington Post laughs a little bit less hard. (Laughter.) Kind of a silence there. (Laughter.) Especially at the Washington Post table. (Laughter.)

GOP Chairman Reince Priebus is here as well. (Applause.) Glad to see you that you feel that you've earned a night off. (Laughter.) Congratulations on all your success. The Republican Party, the nomination process –– it's all going great. Keep it up. (Laughter and applause.)

Kendall Jenner is also here. And we had a chance to meet her backstage –– she seems like a very nice young woman. I'm not exactly sure what she does, but I am told that my Twitter mentions are about to go through the roof. (Laughter.)

Helen Mirren is here tonight. (Applause.) I don't even have a joke here. I just think Helen Mirren is awesome. (Laughter and applause.) She's awesome. (Laughter.)

Sitting at the same table, I see Mike Bloomberg. (Applause.) Mike, a combative, controversial New York billionaire is leading the GOP primary and it is not you. (Laughter.) That's has to sting a little bit. (Laughter.) Although it's not an entirely fair comparison between you and the Donald. After all, Mike was a big-city mayor. He knows policy in depth. And he's actually worth the amount of money that he says he is. (Laughter and applause.)

What an election season. For example, we've got the bright new face of the Democratic Party here tonight

-- Mr. Bernie Sanders! (Applause.) There he is -- Bernie! (Applause.) Bernie, you look like a million bucks. (Laughter.) Or to put it in terms you'll understand, you look like 37,000 donations of 27 dollars each. (Laughter and applause.)

A lot of folks have been surprised by the Bernie phenomenon, especially his appeal to young people. But not me, I get it. Just recently, a young person came up to me and said she was sick of politicians standing in the way of her dreams. As if we were actually going to let Malia go to Burning Man this year. (Laughter.) That was not going to happen. (Laughter.) Bernie might have let her go. (Laughter.) Not us. (Laughter.)

I am hurt, though, Bernie, that you've distancing yourself a little from me. (Laughter.) I mean, that's just not something that you do to your comrade. (Laughter and applause.)

Bernie's slogan has helped his campaign catch fire among young people. "Feel the Bern." (Laughter.) Feel the Bern -- it's a good slogan. Hillary's slogan has not had the same effect. Let's see this. (Slide is shown.) (Laughter.)

Look, I've said how much I admire Hillary's toughness, her smarts, her policy chops, her experience. You've got to admit it, though, Hillary trying to appeal to young voters is a little bit like your relative just signed up for Facebook. (Laughter.) "Dear America, did you get my poke?" (Laughter.) "Is it appearing on your wall?" (Laughter.) "I'm not sure I am using this right. Love, Aunt Hillary."

(Laughter and applause.) It's not entirely persuasive.

Meanwhile, on the Republican side, things are a little more -- how should we say this -- a little "more loose." Just look at the confusion over the invitations to tonight's dinner. Guests were asked to check whether they wanted steak or fish, but instead, a whole bunch of you wrote in Paul Ryan. (Laughter.) That's not an option, people. Steak or fish. (Laughter.) You may not like steak or fish -- (laughter) -- but that's your choice. (Laughter.)

Meanwhile, some candidates aren't polling high enough to qualify for their own joke tonight. (Slide is shown.) (Laughter.) The rules were well-established ahead of time. (Laughter.)

And then there's Ted Cruz. Ted had a tough week. He went to Indiana -- Hoosier country -- stood on a basketball court, and called the hoop a "basketball ring." (Laughter and applause.) What else is in his lexicon? Baseball sticks? Football hats? (Laughter.) But sure, I'm the foreign one. (Laughter and applause.)

Well, let me conclude tonight on a more serious note. I want to thank the Washington press corps, I want to thank Carol for all that you do. The free press is central to our democracy, and -- nah, I'm just kidding! You know I've got to talk about Trump! Come on! (Laughter and applause.) We weren't just going to stop there. Come on. (Laughter and applause.)

Although I am a little hurt that he's not here tonight.

We had so much fun the last time. (Laughter.) And it is surprising. You've got a room full of reporters, celebrities, cameras, and he says no? (Laughter.) Is this dinner too tacky for The Donald? (Laughter.) What could he possibly be doing instead? Is he at home, eating a Trump Steak -- (laughter) -- tweeting out insults to Angela Merkel? (Laughter.) What's he doing? (Laughter.)

The Republican establishment is incredulous that he is their most likely nominee -- incredulous, shocking. They say Donald lacks the foreign policy experience to be President. But, in fairness, he has spent years meeting with leaders from around the world: Miss Sweden, Miss Argentina, Miss Azerbaijan. (Laughter and applause.)

And there's one area where Donald's experience could be invaluable -- and that's closing Guantanamo. Because Trump knows a thing or two about running waterfront properties into the ground. (Laughter and applause.)

All right, that's probably enough. I mean, I've got more material -- (applause) -- no, no, I don't want to spend too much time on The Donald. Following your lead, I want to show some restraint. (Laughter.) Because I think we can all agree that from the start, he's gotten the appropriate amount of coverage, befitting the seriousness of his candidacy. (Laughter and applause.)

I hope you all are proud of yourselves. (Laughter.) The guy wanted to give his hotel business a boost, and now we're praying that Cleveland makes it through July. (Laughter.)

Mm-mm-mm. (Laughter and applause.) Hmm. (Laughter.)

As for me and Michelle, we've decided to stay in D.C. for a couple more years. (Applause.) Thank you. This way, our youngest daughter can finish up high school, Michelle can stay closer to her plot of carrots. (Laughter.) She's already making plans to see them every day. Take a look. (Slide is shown.) (Laughter.)

But our decision has actually presented a bit of a dilemma because, traditionally, Presidents don't stick around after they're done. And it's something that I've been brooding about a little bit. Take a look. (Video is shown.)
(Applause.)

I am still waiting for all of you to respond to my invitation to connect on LinkedIn. (Laughter.) But I know you have jobs to do, which is what really brings us here tonight.

I know that there are times that we've had differences, and that's inherent in our institutional roles -- it's true of every President and his press corps. But we've always shared the same goal -- to root our public discourse in the truth; to open the doors of this democracy; to do whatever we can to make our country and our world more free and more just. And I've always appreciated the role that you have all played as equal partners in reaching these goals.

And our free press is why we once again recognize the real journalists who uncovered a horrifying scandal and brought about some measure of justice for thousands of victims throughout the world. They are here with us tonight –– Sacha Pfeiffer, Mike Rezendes, Walter Robinson, Matt Carroll, and Ben Bradlee, Jr. Please give them a big round of applause. (Applause.)

Our free press is why, once again, we honor Jason Rezaian. (Applause.) As Carol noted, last time this year, we spoke of Jason's courage as he endured the isolation of an Iranian prison. This year, we see that courage in the flesh and it's a living testament to the very idea of a free press, and a reminder of the rising level of danger, and political intimidation, and physical threats faced by reporters overseas. And I can make this commitment that as long as I hold this office, my administration will continue to fight for the release of American journalists held against their will –– and we will not stop until they see the same freedom as Jason had. (Applause.)

At home and abroad, journalists like all of you engage in the dogged pursuit of informing citizens, and holding leaders accountable, and making our government of the people possible. And it's an enormous responsibility. And I realize it's an enormous challenge at a time when the economics of the business sometimes incentivize speed over depth; and when controversy and conflict are what most immediately attract readers and viewers.

The good news is there are so many of you that are pushing against those trends. And as a citizen of this great democracy, I am grateful for that. For this is also a time around the world when some of the fundamental ideals of liberal democracies are under attack, and when notions of objectivity, and of a free press, and of facts, and of evidence are trying to be undermined. Or, in some cases, ignored entirely.

And in such a climate, it's not enough just to give people a megaphone. And that's why your power and your responsibility to dig and to question and to counter distortions and untruths is more important than ever. Taking a stand on behalf of what is true does not require you shedding your objectivity. In fact, it is the essence of good journalism. It affirms the idea that the only way we can build consensus, the only way that we can move forward as a country, the only way we can help the world mend itself is by agreeing on a baseline of facts when it comes to the challenges that confront us all.

So this night is a testament to all of you who have devoted your lives to that idea, who push to shine a light on the truth every single day. So I want to close my final White House Correspondents' Dinner by just saying thank you. (Applause.) I'm very proud of what you've done. It has been an honor and a privilege to work side by side with you to strengthen our democracy. (Applause.)

And with that, I just have two more words to say --
Obama out. (Drops microphone.) (Laughter and applause.) Thank you. (Applause.)

14 "I'm asking you to believe. Not in my ability to bring about change – but in yours."

Farewell Address
10 January 2017
Chicago, Illinois

Barack Obama's farewell address is the final public speech of Barack Obama as the 44th President of the United States, broadcast on various television and radio stations and live streamed online by the White House.

Hello, Chicago! It's good to be home! Thank you, everybody. Thank you. Thank you so much. Thank you. All right, everybody sit down. We're on live TV here. I've got to move. You can tell that I'm a lame duck because nobody is following instructions. Everybody have a seat.

My fellow Americans -- Michelle and I have been so touched by all the well wishes that we've received over the past few weeks. But tonight, it's my turn to say thanks. Whether we have seen eye-to-eye or rarely agreed at all, my conversations with you, the American people, in living rooms and in schools, at farms, on factory floors, at diners and on distant military outposts those conversations are what have kept me honest, and kept me inspired, and kept me going. And every day, I have learned from you. You made me a better President, and you made me a better man.

So I first came to Chicago when I was in my early 20s. And I was still trying to figure out who I was, still searching for a purpose in my life. And it was a neighborhood not far from here where I began working with church groups in the shadows of closed steel mills. It was on these streets where I witnessed the power of faith, and the quiet dignity of working people in the face of struggle and loss.

AUDIENCE: Four more years! Four more years! Four more years!

I can't do that.

Four more years! Four more years! Four more years!

This is where I learned that change only happens when ordinary people get involved and they get engaged, and they come together to demand it.

After eight years as your President, I still believe that. And it's not just my belief. It's the beating heart of our American idea -- our bold experiment in self-government. It's the conviction that we are all created equal, endowed by our Creator with certain unalienable rights, among them life, liberty, and the pursuit of happiness. It's the insistence that these rights, while self-evident, have never been self-executing; that We, the People, through the instrument of our democracy, can form a more perfect union.

What a radical idea. A great gift that our Founders gave to us: The freedom to chase our individual dreams through our sweat and toil and imagination, and the imperative to strive together, as well, to achieve a common good, a greater good.

For 240 years, our nation's call to citizenship has given work and purpose to each new generation. It's what led patriots to choose republic over tyranny, pioneers to trek west, slaves to brave that makeshift railroad to freedom. It's what pulled immigrants and refugees across oceans and the Rio Grande. It's what pushed women to reach for the ballot. It's what powered workers to organize. It's why GIs gave their lives at Omaha Beach and Iwo Jima, Iraq and Afghanistan. And why men and women from Selma to Stonewall were prepared to give theirs, as well.

So that's what we mean when we say America is exceptional -- not that our nation has been flawless from the start, but that we have shown the capacity to change and make life better for those who follow. Yes, our progress has been uneven. The work of democracy has always been hard. It's always been contentious. Sometimes it's been bloody. For every two steps forward, it often feels we take one step back. But the long sweep of America has been defined by forward motion, a constant widening of our founding creed to embrace all and not just some.

If I had told you eight years ago that America would reverse a great recession, reboot our auto industry, and unleash the longest stretch of job creation in our history -- if I had told you that we would open up a new chapter with the Cuban people, shut down Iran's nuclear weapons program without firing a shot, take out the mastermind of 9/11 -- if I had told you that we would win marriage equality, and secure the right to health insurance for another 20 million of our fellow citizens -- if I had told you all that, you might have said our sights were set a little too high. But that's what we did. That's what you did.

You were the change. You answered people's hopes, and because of you, by almost every measure, America is a better, stronger place than it was when we started.

In 10 days, the world will witness a hallmark of our democracy.

AUDIENCE: Noooo --

No, no, no, no, no -- the peaceful transfer of power from one freely elected President to the next. I committed to President-elect Trump that my administration would ensure the smoothest possible transition, just as President Bush did for me. Because it's up to all of us to make sure our government can help us meet the many challenges we still face.

We have what we need to do so. We have everything

we need to meet those challenges. After all, we remain the wealthiest, most powerful, and most respected nation on Earth. Our youth, our drive, our diversity and openness, our boundless capacity for risk and reinvention means that the future should be ours. But that potential will only be realized if our democracy works. Only if our politics better reflects the decency of our people. Only if all of us, regardless of party affiliation or particular interests, help restore the sense of common purpose that we so badly need right now.

That's what I want to focus on tonight: The state of our democracy. Understand, democracy does not require uniformity. Our founders argued. They quarreled. Eventually they compromised. They expected us to do the same. But they knew that democracy does require a basic sense of solidarity -- the idea that for all our outward differences, we're all in this together; that we rise or fall as one.

There have been moments throughout our history that threatens that solidarity. And the beginning of this century has been one of those times. A shrinking world, growing inequality; demographic change and the specter of terrorism -- these forces haven't just tested our security and our prosperity, but are testing our democracy, as well. And how we meet these challenges to our democracy will determine our ability to educate our kids, and create good jobs, and protect our homeland. In other words, it will determine our future.

To begin with, our democracy won't work without a sense that everyone has economic opportunity. And the good news is that today the economy is growing again. Wages, incomes, home values, and retirement accounts are all rising again. Poverty is falling again. The wealthy are paying a fairer share of taxes even as the stock market shatters records. The unemployment rate is near a 10-year low. The uninsured rate has never, ever been lower. Health care costs are rising at the slowest rate in 50 years. And I've said and I mean it -- if anyone can put together a plan that is demonstrably better than the improvements we've made to our health care system and that covers as many people at less cost, I will publicly support it.

Because that, after all, is why we serve. Not to score points or take credit, but to make people's lives better.

But for all the real progress that we've made, we know it's not enough. Our economy doesn't work as well or grow as fast when a few prosper at the expense of a growing middle class and ladders for folks who want to get into the middle class. That's the economic argument. But stark inequality is also corrosive to our democratic ideal. While the top one percent has amassed a bigger share of wealth and income, too many families, in inner cities and in rural counties, have been left behind -- the laid-off factory worker; the waitress or health care worker who's just barely getting by and struggling to pay the bills -- convinced that the game is fixed against them, that their government only serves the interests of the powerful -- that's a recipe for more cynicism and polarization in our politics.

But there are no quick fixes to this long-term trend. I agree, our trade should be fair and not just free. But the next wave of economic dislocations won't come from overseas. It will come from the relentless pace of automation that makes a lot of good, middle-class jobs obsolete.

And so we're going to have to forge a new social compact to guarantee all our kids the education they need -- to give workers the power to unionize for better wages; to update the social safety net to reflect the way we live now, and make more reforms to the tax code so corporations and individuals who reap the most from this new economy don't avoid their obligations to the country that's made their very success possible.

We can argue about how to best achieve these goals. But we can't be complacent about the goals themselves. For if we don't create opportunity for all people, the disaffection and division that has stalled our progress will only sharpen in years to come.

There's a second threat to our democracy -- and this one is as old as our nation itself. After my election, there was talk of a post-racial America. And such a vision, however well-intended, was never realistic. Race remains a potent and often divisive force in our society. Now, I've lived long enough to know that race relations are better than they were 10, or 20, or 30 years ago, no matter what some folks say. You can see it not just in statistics, you see it in the attitudes of young Americans across the political spectrum.

But we're not where we need to be. And all of us have more work to do. If every economic issue is framed as a struggle between a hardworking white middle class and an undeserving minority, then workers of all shades are going to be left fighting for scraps while the wealthy withdraw further into their private enclaves. If we're unwilling to invest in the children of immigrants, just because they don't look like us, we will diminish the prospects of our own children -- because those brown kids will represent a larger and larger share of America's workforce. And we have shown that our economy doesn't have to be a zero-sum game. Last year, incomes rose for all races, all age groups, for men and for women.

So if we're going to be serious about race going forward, we need to uphold laws against discrimination -- in hiring, and in housing, and in education, and in the criminal justice system. That is what our Constitution and our highest ideals require.

But laws alone won't be enough. Hearts must change. It won't change overnight. Social attitudes oftentimes take generations to change. But if our democracy is to work in this increasingly diverse nation, then each one of us need to try to heed the advice of a great character in American fiction -- Atticus Finch -- who said "You never really understand a person until you consider things from his point of view...until you climb into his skin and walk around in it."

For blacks and other minority groups, it means tying our own very real struggles for justice to the challenges that a lot of people in this country face --

not only the refugee, or the immigrant, or the rural poor, or the transgender American, but also the middle-aged white guy who, from the outside, may seem like he's got advantages, but has seen his world upended by economic and cultural and technological change. We have to pay attention, and listen.

For white Americans, it means acknowledging that the effects of slavery and Jim Crow didn't suddenly vanish in the '60s -- that when minority groups voice discontent, they're not just engaging in reverse racism or practicing political correctness. When they wage peaceful protest, they're not demanding special treatment but the equal treatment that our Founders promised.

For native-born Americans, it means reminding ourselves that the stereotypes about immigrants today were said, almost word for word, about the Irish, and Italians, and Poles -- who it was said we're going to destroy the fundamental character of America. And as it turned out, America wasn't weakened by the presence of these newcomers; these newcomers embraced this nation's creed, and this nation was strengthened.

So regardless of the station that we occupy, we all have to try harder. We all have to start with the premise that each of our fellow citizens loves this country just as much as we do; that they value hard work and family just like we do; that their children are just as curious and hopeful and worthy of love as our own.

And that's not easy to do. For too many of us, it's

become safer to retreat into our own bubbles, whether in our neighborhoods or on college campuses, or places of worship, or especially our social media feeds, surrounded by people who look like us and share the same political outlook and never challenge our assumptions. The rise of naked partisanship, and increasing economic and regional stratification, the splintering of our media into a channel for every taste -- all this makes this great sorting seem natural, even inevitable. And increasingly, we become so secure in our bubbles that we start accepting only information, whether it's true or not, that fits our opinions, instead of basing our opinions on the evidence that is out there.

And this trend represents a third threat to our democracy. But politics is a battle of ideas. That's how our democracy was designed. In the course of a healthy debate, we prioritize different goals, and the different means of reaching them. But without some common baseline of facts, without a willingness to admit new information, and concede that your opponent might be making a fair point, and that science and reason matter -- then we're going to keep talking past each other, and we'll make common ground and compromise impossible.

And isn't that part of what so often makes politics dispiriting? How can elected officials rage about deficits when we propose to spend money on preschool for kids, but not when we're cutting taxes for corporations? How do we excuse ethical lapses in our own party, but pounce when the other party does the same thing? It's not just dishonest, this selective sorting of the facts; it's self-defeating. Because, as my mother used to tell me, reality has a way of catching up with you.

Take the challenge of climate change. In just eight years, we've halved our dependence on foreign oil; we've doubled our renewable energy; we've led the world to an agreement that has the promise to save this planet. But without bolder action, our children won't have time to debate the existence of climate change. They'll be busy dealing with its effects: more environmental disasters, more economic disruptions, waves of climate refugees seeking sanctuary.

Now, we can and should argue about the best approach to solve the problem. But to simply deny the problem not only betrays future generations, it betrays the essential spirit of this country -- the essential spirit of innovation and practical problem-solving that guided our Founders.

It is that spirit, born of the Enlightenment, that made us an economic powerhouse -- the spirit that took flight at Kitty Hawk and Cape Canaveral; the spirit that cures disease and put a computer in every pocket.

It's that spirit -- a faith in reason, and enterprise, and the primacy of right over might -- that allowed us to resist the lure of fascism and tyranny during the Great Depression; that allowed us to build a post-World War II order with other democracies, an order based not just on military power or national affiliations but built on principles -- the rule of law, human rights, freedom of religion, and speech, and assembly, and an independent press.

That order is now being challenged -- first by violent fanatics who claim to speak for Islam; more recently by autocrats in foreign capitals who see free markets and open democracies and and civil society itself as a threat to their power. The peril each poses to our democracy is more far-reaching than a car bomb or a missile. It represents the fear of change; the fear of people who look or speak or pray differently; a contempt for the rule of law that holds leaders accountable; an intolerance of dissent and free thought; a belief that the sword or the gun or the bomb or the propaganda machine is the ultimate arbiter of what's true and what's right.

Because of the extraordinary courage of our men and women in uniform, because of our intelligence officers, and law enforcement, and diplomats who support our troops -- no foreign terrorist organization has successfully planned and executed an attack on our homeland these past eight years. And although Boston and Orlando and San Bernardino and Fort Hood remind us of how dangerous radicalization can be, our law enforcement agencies are more effective and vigilant than ever. We have taken out tens of thousands of terrorists -- including bin Laden. The global coalition we're leading against ISIL has taken out their leaders, and taken away about half their territory. ISIL will be destroyed, and no one who threatens America will ever be safe.

And to all who serve or have served, it has been the honor of my lifetime to be your Commander-in-Chief. And we all owe you a deep debt of gratitude.

But protecting our way of life, that's not just the job of our military. Democracy can buckle when we give in to fear. So, just as we, as citizens, must remain vigilant against external aggression, we must guard against a weakening of the values that make us who we are.

And that's why, for the past eight years, I've worked to put the fight against terrorism on a firmer legal footing. That's why we've ended torture, worked to close Gitmo, reformed our laws governing surveillance to protect privacy and civil liberties. That's why I reject discrimination against Muslim Americans, who are just as patriotic as we are.

That's why we cannot withdraw from big global fights -- to expand democracy, and human rights, and women's rights, and LGBT rights. No matter how imperfect our efforts, no matter how expedient ignoring such values may seem, that's part of defending America. For the fight against extremism and intolerance and sectarianism and chauvinism are of a piece with the fight against authoritarianism and nationalist aggression. If the scope of freedom and respect for the rule of law shrinks around the world, the likelihood of war within and between nations increases, and our own freedoms will eventually be threatened.

So let's be vigilant, but not afraid. ISIL will try to kill innocent people. But they cannot defeat America unless we betray our Constitution and our principles in the fight. Rivals like Russia or China cannot match our influence around the world -- unless we give up what we stand for -- and turn ourselves into just another big country that bullies smaller neighbors.

Which brings me to my final point: Our democracy is threatened whenever we take it for granted. All of us, regardless of party, should be throwing ourselves into the task of rebuilding our democratic institutions. When voting rates in America are some of the lowest among advanced democracies, we should be making it easier, not harder, to vote. When trust in our institutions is low, we should reduce the corrosive influence of money in our politics, and insist on the principles of transparency and ethics in public service. When Congress is dysfunctional, we should draw our congressional districts to encourage politicians to cater to common sense and not rigid extremes.

But remember, none of this happens on its own. All of this depends on our participation; on each of us accepting the responsibility of citizenship, regardless of which way the pendulum of power happens to be swinging.

Our Constitution is a remarkable, beautiful gift. But it's really just a piece of parchment. It has no power on its own. We, the people, give it power. We, the people, give it meaning. With our participation, and with the choices that we make, and the alliances that we forge. Whether or not we stand up for our freedoms. Whether or not we respect and enforce the rule of law. That's up to us. America is no fragile thing. But the gains of our long journey to freedom are not assured.

In his own farewell address, George Washington wrote that self-government is the underpinning of our safety, prosperity, and liberty, but "from different causes and from different quarters much pains will be taken...to weaken in your minds the conviction of this truth." And so we have to preserve this truth with "jealous anxiety;" that we should reject "the first dawning of every attempt to alienate any portion of our country from the rest or to enfeeble the sacred ties" that make us one.

America, we weaken those ties when we allow our political dialogue to become so corrosive that people of good character aren't even willing to enter into public service; so coarse with rancor that Americans with whom we disagree are seen not just as misguided but as malevolent. We weaken those ties when we define some of us as more American than others; when we write off the whole system as inevitably corrupt, and when we sit back and blame the leaders we elect without examining our own role in electing them.

It falls to each of us to be those those anxious, jealous guardians of our democracy; to embrace the joyous task we've been given to continually try to improve this great nation of ours. Because for all our outward differences, we, in fact, all share the same proud title, the most important office in a democracy: Citizen. Citizen.

So, you see, that's what our democracy demands. It needs you. Not just when there's an election, not just when your own narrow interest is at stake, but over the full span of a lifetime. If you're tired of arguing with strangers on the Internet, try talking with one of them in real life. If something needs fixing, then lace up your shoes and do some organizing. If you're disappointed by your elected officials, grab a clipboard, get some signatures, and run for office yourself. Show up. Dive in. Stay at it.

Sometimes you'll win. Sometimes you'll lose. Presuming a reservoir of goodness in other people, that can be a risk, and there will be times when the process will disappoint you. But for those of us fortunate enough to have been a part of this work, and to see it up close, let me tell you, it can energize and inspire. And more often than not, your faith in America -- and in Americans -- will be confirmed.

Mine sure has been. Over the course of these eight years, I've seen the hopeful faces of young graduates and our newest military officers. I have mourned with grieving families searching for answers, and found grace in a Charleston church. I've seen our scientists help a paralyzed man regain his sense of touch. I've seen wounded warriors who at points were given up for dead walk again. I've seen our doctors and volunteers rebuild after earthquakes and stop pandemics in their tracks. I've seen the youngest of children remind us through their actions and through their generosity of our obligations to care for refugees, or work for peace, and, above all, to look out for each other.

So that faith that I placed all those years ago, not far from here, in the power of ordinary Americans to bring about change -- that faith has been rewarded in ways I could not have possibly imagined. And I hope your faith has, too. Some of you here tonight or watching at home, you were there with us in 2004, in 2008, 2012 -- maybe you still can't believe we pulled this whole thing off. Let me tell you, you're not the only ones.

Michelle -- Michelle LaVaughn Robinson, girl of the South Side -- for the past 25 years, you have not only been my wife and mother of my children, you have been my best friend. You took on a role you didn't ask for and you made it your own, with grace and with grit and with style and good humor. You made the White House a place that belongs to everybody. And the new generation sets its sights higher because it has you as a role model. So you have made me proud. And you have made the country proud.

Malia and Sasha, under the strangest of circumstances, you have become two amazing young women. You are smart and you are beautiful, but more importantly, you are kind and you are thoughtful and you are full of passion. (Applause.) You wore the burden of years in the spotlight so easily. Of all that I've done in my life, I am most proud to be your dad.

To Joe Biden -- the scrappy kid from Scranton who became Delaware's favorite son -- you were the first decision I made as a nominee, and it was the best. Not just because you have been a great Vice President, but because in the bargain, I gained a brother. And we love you and Jill like family, and your friendship has been one of the great joys of our lives.

To my remarkable staff: For eight years -- and for some of you, a whole lot more -- I have drawn from your energy, and every day I tried to reflect back what you displayed -- heart, and character, and idealism. I've watched you grow up, get married, have kids, start incredible new journeys of your own. Even when times got tough and frustrating, you never let Washington get the better of you. You guarded against cynicism. And the only thing that makes me prouder than all the good that we've done is the thought of all the amazing things that you're going to achieve from here.

And to all of you out there -- every organizer who moved to an unfamiliar town, every kind family who welcomed them in, every volunteer who knocked on doors, every young person who cast a ballot for the first time, every American who lived and breathed the hard work of change -- you are the best supporters and organizers anybody could ever hope for, and I will be forever grateful. Because you did change the world. You did.

And that's why I leave this stage tonight even more optimistic about this country than when we started. Because I know our work has not only helped so many Americans, it has inspired so many Americans -- especially so many young people out there -- to believe that you can make a difference -- to hitch your wagon to something bigger than yourselves.

Let me tell you, this generation coming up -- unselfish, altruistic, creative, patriotic -- I've seen you in every corner of the country. You believe in a fair, and just, and inclusive America. You know that constant change has been America's hallmark; that it's not something to fear but something to embrace. You are willing to carry this hard work of democracy forward. You'll soon outnumber all of us, and I believe as a result the future is in good hands.

My fellow Americans, it has been the honor of my life to serve you. I won't stop. In fact, I will be right there with you, as a citizen, for all my remaining days. But for now, whether you are young or whether you're young at heart, I do have one final ask of you as your President -- the same thing I asked when you took a chance on me eight years ago. I'm asking you to believe. Not in my ability to bring about change -- but in yours.

I am asking you to hold fast to that faith written into our founding documents; that idea whispered by slaves and abolitionists; that spirit sung by immigrants and homesteaders and those who marched for justice; that creed reaffirmed by those who planted flags from foreign battlefields to the surface of the moon; a creed at the core of every American whose story is not yet written: Yes, we can.

Yes, we did. Yes, we can.

Thank you. God bless you. May God continue to bless the United States of America.

15 "It did not start with Donald Trump. He is a symptom, not the cause."

Accepting the Paul H. Douglas Award for Ethics in Government
September 7, 2018
University of Illinois, Ubana, Illinois

The former president speaks about President Trump, by name, and Republicans in Congress, while urging students in the audience to vote in an election he called a turning point.

PRESIDENT OBAMA: Hey! Hello, Illinois! I–L–L!
AUDIENCE: I–L–L!
PRESIDENT OBAMA: I–L–L!
AUDIENCE: I–L–L!
PRESIDENT OBAMA: I–L–L!
AUDIENCE: I–L–L!

Okay, okay. Just checking to see if you're awake.
Please have a seat, everybody. It is good to be home.

It's good to see corn. (Laughter.)

Beans. I was trying to explain to somebody as we were flying in, that's corn. That's beans. And they were very impressed at my agricultural knowledge. Please give it up for Amaury once again for that outstanding introduction. I have a bunch of good friends here today, including somebody who I served with, who is one of the finest senators in the country, and we're lucky to have him, your Senator, Dick Durbin is here. I also noticed, by the way, former Governor Edgar here, who I haven't seen in a long time, and somehow he has not aged and I have. And it's great to see you, Governor. I want to thank President Killeen and everybody at the U of I System for making it possible for me to be here today. And I am deeply honored at the Paul Douglas Award that is being given to me. He is somebody who set the path for so much outstanding public service here in Illinois.

Now, I want to start by addressing the elephant in the room. I know people are still wondering why I didn't speak at the commencement. (Laughter.)

The student body president sent a very thoughtful invitation. The students made a spiffy video. And when I declined, I hear there was speculation that I was boycotting campus until Antonio's Pizza reopened. (Laughter.)

So I want to be clear. I did not take sides in that late-night food debate. The truth is, after eight years in the White House, I needed to spend some time one-on-one with Michelle if I wanted to stay married.

(Laughter.)

And she says hello, by the way. I also wanted to spend some quality time with my daughters, who were suddenly young women on their way out the door. And I should add, by the way, now that I have a daughter in college, I can tell all the students here, your parents suffer. (Laughter.)

They cry privately. It is brutal. So please call. (Laughter.)

Send a text. (Applause.)

We need to hear from you, just a little something. And truth was, I was also intent on following a wise American tradition. Of ex-presidents gracefully exiting the political stage, making room for new voices and new ideas. And we have our first president, George Washington, to thank for setting that example. After he led the colonies to victory as General Washington, there were no constraints on him really, he was practically a god to those who had followed him into battle.

There was no Constitution, there were no democratic norms that guided what he should or could do. And he could have made himself all-powerful, he could have made himself potentially President for life. And instead he resigned as Commander-in-Chief and moved back to his country estate. Six years later, he was elected President. But after two terms, he resigned again, and rode off into the sunset.

The point Washington made, the point that is

essential to American democracy, is that in a government of and by and for the people, there should be no permanent ruling class. There are only citizens, who through their elected and temporary representatives, determine our course and determine our character.

I'm here today because this is one of those pivotal moments when every one of us, as citizens of the United States, need to determine just who it is that we are, just what it is that we stand for. And as a fellow citizen, not as an ex-president, but as a fellow citizen, I am here to deliver a simple message, and that is that you need to vote because our democracy depends on it. (Applause.)

Now, some of you may think I'm exaggerating when I say this November's elections are more important than any I can remember in my lifetime. I know politicians say that all the time. I have been guilty of saying it a few times, particularly when I was on the ballot. (Laughter.)

But just a glance at recent headlines should tell you that this moment really is different. The stakes really are higher. The consequences of any of us sitting on the sidelines are more dire. And it's not as if we haven't had big elections before or big choices to make in our history.

The fact is, democracy has never been easy, and our founding fathers argued about everything. We waged a civil war. We overcame depression. We've lurched from eras of great progressive change to periods of retrenchment. Still, most Americans alive today, certainly the students who are here, have operated under some common assumptions about who we are and what we stand for.

Out of the turmoil of the industrial revolution and the Great Depression, America adapted a new economy, a 20th century economy - guiding our free market with regulations to protect health and safety and fair competition, empowering workers with union movements; investing in science and infrastructure and educational institutions like U of I; strengthening our system of primary and secondary education, and stitching together a social safety net. And all of this led to unrivaled prosperity and the rise of a broad and deep middle class in the sense that if you worked hard, you could climb the ladder of success.

And not everyone was included in this prosperity. There was a lot more work to do. And so in response to the stain of slavery and segregation and the reality of racial discrimination, the civil rights movement not only opened new doors for African-Americans, it also opened up the floodgates of opportunity for women and Americans with disabilities and LGBT Americans and others to make their own claims to full and equal citizenship.

And although discrimination remained a pernicious force in our society and continues to this day, and although there are controversies about how to best ensure genuine equality of opportunity, there's been at least rough agreement among the overwhelming majority of Americans that our country is strongest when everybody's treated fairly, when people are judged on the merits and the content of their character, and not the color of their skin or the way in which they worship God or their last names. And that consensus then extended beyond our borders. And from the wreckage of World War II, we built a postwar web, architecture, system of alliances and institutions to underwrite freedom and oppose Soviet totalitarianism and to help poorer countries develop.

This American leadership across the globe wasn't perfect. We made mistakes. At times we lost sight of our ideals. We had fierce arguments about Vietnam, and we had fierce arguments about Iraq. But thanks to our leadership, a bipartisan leadership, and the efforts of diplomats and Peace Corps volunteers, and most of all thanks to the constant sacrifices of our men and women in uniform, we not only reduced the prospects of war between the world's great powers, we not only won the Cold War, we helped spread a commitment to certain values and principles, like the rule of law and human rights and democracy and the notion of the inherent dignity and worth of every individual.

And even those countries that didn't abide by those principles were still subject to shame and still had to at least give lip service to the idea. And that provided a lever to continually improve the prospects for people around the world.

That's the story of America. A story of progress. Fitful progress, incomplete progress, but progress. And that progress wasn't achieved by just a handful of famous leaders making speeches. It was won because of countless quiet acts of heroism and dedication by citizens, by ordinary people, many of them not much older than you. It was won because rather than be bystanders to history, ordinary people fought and marched and mobilized and built and, yes, voted to make history.

Of course, there's always been another darker aspect to America's story. Progress doesn't just move in a straight line. There's a reason why progress hasn't been easy and why throughout our history every two steps forward seems to sometimes produce one step back.

Each time we painstakingly pull ourselves closer to our founding ideals, that all of us are created equal, endowed by our Creator with certain inalienable rights; the ideals that say every child should have opportunity and every man and woman in this country who's willing to work hard should be able to find a job and support a family and pursue their small piece of the American Dream; our ideals that say we have a collective responsibility to care for the sick and the infirm, and we have a responsibility to conserve the amazing bounty, the natural resources of this country and of this planet for future generations, each time we've gotten closer to those ideals, somebody somewhere has pushed back. The status quo pushes back.

Sometimes the backlash comes from people who are genuinely, if wrongly, fearful of change. More often it's manufactured by the powerful and the privileged who want to keep us divided and keep us angry and keep us cynical because that helps them maintain the status quo and keep their power and keep their privilege. And you happen to be coming of age during one of those moments. It did not start with Donald Trump. He is a symptom, not the cause. (Applause.)

He's just capitalizing on resentments that politicians have been fanning for years. A fear and anger that's rooted in our past, but it's also born out of the enormous upheavals that have taken place in your brief lifetimes.

And, by the way, it is brief. When I heard Amaury was eleven when I got elected, and now Amaury's starting a company, that was yesterday. But think about it. You've come of age in a smaller, more connected world, where demographic shifts and the winds of change have scrambled not only traditional economic arrangements, but our social arrangements and our religious commitments and our civic institutions.

Most of you don't remember a time before 9/11, when you didn't have to take off your shoes at an airport. Most of you don't remember a time when America wasn't at war, or when money and images and information could travel instantly around the globe, or when the climate wasn't changing faster than our efforts to address it. This change has happened fast, faster than any time in human history. And it created a new economy that has unleashed incredible prosperity.

But it's also upended people's lives in profound ways. For those with unique skills or access to technology and capital, a global market has meant unprecedented wealth. For those not so lucky, for the factory worker, for the office worker, or even middle managers, those same forces may have wiped out your job, or at least put you in no position to ask for a raise. As wages slowed and inequality accelerated, those at the top of the economic pyramid have been able to influence government to skew things even more in their direction: cutting taxes on the wealthiest Americans, unwinding regulations and weakening worker protections, shrinking the safety net.

So you have come of age during a time of growing inequality, of fracturing of economic opportunity. And that growing economic divide compounded other divisions in our country: regional, racial, religious, cultural. It made it harder to build consensus on issues. It made politicians less willing to compromise, which increased gridlock, which made people even more cynical about politics.

And then the reckless behavior of financial elites triggered a massive financial crisis, ten years ago this week, a crisis that resulted in the worst recession in any of our lifetimes and caused years of hardship for the American people, for many of your parents, for many of your families.

Most of you weren't old enough to fully focus on what was going on at the time, but when I came into office in 2009, we were losing 800,000 jobs a month. 800,000. Millions of people were losing their homes. Many were worried we were entering into a second Great Depression. So we worked hard to end that crisis, but also to break some of these longer term trends. And the actions we took during that crisis returned the economy to healthy growth and initiated the longest streak of job creation on record. And we covered another 20 million Americans with health insurance and we cut our deficits by more than half, partly by making sure that people like me, who have been given such amazing opportunities by this country, pay our fair share of taxes to help folks coming up behind me.

And by the time I left office, household income was near its all-time high and the uninsured rate had hit an all-time low and wages were rising and poverty rates were falling. I mention all this just so when you hear how great the economy's doing right now, let's just remember when this recovery started.

I mean, I'm glad it's continued, but when you hear about this economic miracle that's been going on, when the job numbers come out, monthly job numbers, suddenly Republicans are saying it's a miracle. I have to kind of remind them, actually, those job numbers are the same as they were in 2015 and 2016.

Anyway, I digress. So we made progress, but -- and this is the truth -- my administration couldn't reverse forty-year trends in only eight years, especially once Republicans took over the House of Representatives in and decided to block everything we did, even things they used to support.

So we pulled the economy out of crisis, but to this day, too many people who once felt solidly middle-class still feel very real and very personal economic insecurity. Even though we took out bin Laden and wound down the wars in Iraq and our combat role in Afghanistan, and got Iran to halt its nuclear program, the world's still full of threats and disorder.

That comes streaming through people's televisions every single day. And these challenges get people worried. And it frays our civic trust. And it makes a lot of people feel like the fix is in and the game is rigged, and nobody's looking out for them. Especially those communities outside our big urban centers.

And even though your generation is the most diverse in history, with a greater acceptance and celebration of our differences than ever before, those are the kinds of conditions that are ripe for exploitation by politicians who have no compunction and no shame about tapping into America's dark history of racial and ethnic and religious division

Appealing to tribe, appealing to fear, pitting one group against another, telling people that order and security will be restored if it weren't for those who don't look like us or don't sound like us or don't pray like we do, that's an old playbook. It's as old as time. And in a healthy democracy it doesn't work. Our antibodies kick in, and people of goodwill from across the political spectrum callout the bigots and the fearmongers, and work to compromise and get things done and promote the better angels of our nature.

But when there's a vacuum in our democracy, when we don't vote, when we take our basic rights and freedoms for granted, when we turn away and stop paying attention and stop engaging and stop believing and look for the newest diversion, the electronic versions of bread and circuses, then other voices fill the void.

A politics of fear and resentment and retrenchment takes hold. And demagogues promise simple fixes to complex problems. They promise to fight for the little guy even as they cater to the wealthiest and the most powerful. They promise to clean up corruption and then plunder away. They start undermining norms that ensure accountability, try to change the rules to entrench their power further. And they appeal to racial nationalism that's barely veiled, if veiled at all.

Sound familiar? Now, understand, this is not just a matter of Democrats versus Republicans or liberals versus conservatives. At various times in our history, this kind of politics has infected both parties. Southern Democrats were the bigger defenders of slavery. It took a Republican President, Abraham Lincoln, to end it. Dixiecrats filibustered anti-lynching legislation, opposed the idea of expanding civil rights, and although it was a Democratic President and a majority Democratic Congress, spurred on by young marchers and protestors, that got the Civil Rights Act and the Voting Rights Act over the finish line, those historic laws also got passed because of the leadership of Republicans like Illinois' own Everett Dirksen.

So neither party has had a monopoly on wisdom, neither party has been exclusively responsible for us going backwards instead of forwards. But I have to say this because sometimes we hear, oh, a plague on both your houses. Over the past few decades, it wasn't true when Jim Edgar was governor here in

Illinois or Jim Thompson was governor. I've got a lot of good Republican friends here in Illinois. But over the past few decades, the politics of division, of resentment and paranoia has unfortunately found a home in the Republican Party.

This Congress has championed the unwinding of campaign finance laws to give billionaires outsized influence over our politics; systemically attacked voting rights to make it harder for the young people, the minorities, and the poor to vote.

Handed out tax cuts without regard to deficits. Slashed the safety net wherever it could. Cast dozens of votes to take away health insurance from ordinary Americans. Embraced wild conspiracy theories, like those surrounding Benghazi, or my birth certificate. (Laughter.)

Rejected science, rejected facts on things like climate change. Embraced a rising absolutism from a willingness to default on America's debt by not paying our bills, to a refusal to even meet, much less consider, a qualified nominee for the Supreme Court because he happened to be nominated by a Democratic President. None of this is conservative. I don't mean to pretend I'm channeling Abraham Lincoln now, but that's not what he had in mind, I think, when he helped form the Republican Party.

It's not conservative. It sure isn't normal. It's radical. It's a vision that says the protection of our power and those who back us is all that matters, even when it hurts the country. It's a vision that says the few who can afford a high-priced lobbyist and unlimited campaign contributions set the agenda. And over the past two years, this vision is now nearing its logical conclusion.

So that with Republicans in control of Congress and the White House, without any checks or balances whatsoever, they've provided another $. trillion in tax cuts to people like me who, I promise, don't need it, and don't even pretend to pay for them. It's supposed to be the party, supposedly, of fiscal conservatism. Suddenly deficits do not matter, even though, just two years ago, when the deficit was lower, they said, I couldn't afford to help working families or seniors on Medicare because the deficit was an existential crisis.

What changed? What changed? They're subsidizing corporate polluters with taxpayer dollars, allowing dishonest lenders to take advantage of veterans and students and consumers again. They've made it so that the only nation on earth to pull out of the global climate agreement, it's not North Korea, it's not Syria, it's not Russia or Saudi Arabia. It's us. The only country.There are a lot of countries in the world. We're the only ones.

They're undermining our alliances, cozying up to Russia. What happened to the Republican Party? Its central organizing principle in foreign policy was the fight against Communism, and now they're cozying up to the former head of the KGB, actively blocking legislation that would defend our elections from Russian attack. What happened?

Their sabotage of the Affordable Care Act has already

cost more than three million Americans their health insurance. And if they're still in power next fall, you'd better believe they're coming at it again. They've said so. In a healthy democracy, there's some checks and balances on this kind of behavior, this kind of inconsistency, but right now there's none.

Republicans who know better in Congress -- and they're there, they're quoted saying, Yeah, we know this is kind of crazy - still bending over backwards to shield this behavior from scrutiny or accountability or consequence. Seem utterly unwilling to find the backbone to safeguard the institutions that make our democracy work.

And, by the way, the claim that everything will turn out okay because there are people inside the White House who secretly aren't following the President's orders, that is not a check -- I'm being serious here -- that's not how our democracy is supposed to work.

These people aren't elected. They're not accountable. They're not doing us a service by actively promoting 90 percent of the crazy stuff that's coming out of this White House and then saying, Don't worry, we're preventing the other 10 percent. That's not how things are supposed to work. This is not normal.

These are extraordinary times. And they're dangerous times. But here's the good news. In two months we have the chance, not the certainty but the chance, to restore some semblance of sanity to our politics.

Because there is actually only on real check on bad policy and abuses of power, and that's you. You and your vote. Look, Americans will always have disagreements on policy. This is a big country, it is a raucous country. People have different points of view. I happen to be a Democrat. I support Democratic candidates. I believe our policies are better and that we have a bigger, bolder vision of opportunity and equality and justice and inclusive democracy.

We know there are a lot of jobs young people aren't getting a chance to occupy or aren't getting paid enough or aren't getting benefits like insurance. It's harder for young people to save for a rainy day, let alone retirement. So Democrats aren't just running on good old ideas like a higher minimum wage, they're running on good new ideas like Medicare for all, giving workers seats on corporate boards, reversing the most egregious corporate tax cuts to make sure college students graduate debt-free.

We know that people are tired of toxic corruption, and that democracy depends on transparency and accountability. So Democrats aren't just running on good old ideas like requiring presidential candidates to release their tax returns, and barring lobbyists from making campaign contributions, but on good new ideas like barring lobbyists from getting paid by foreign governments.

We know that climate change isn't just coming. It is here. So Democrats aren't just running on good old ideas like increasing gas mileage in our cars -- which I did and which Republicans are trying to reverse --

but on good new ideas like putting a price on carbon pollution. We know that in a smaller, more connected world, we can't just put technology back in a box, we can't just put walls up all around America. Walls don't keep out threats like terrorism or disease --

-- and that's why we propose leading our alliances and helping other countries develop, and pushing back against tyrants. And Democrats talk about reforming our immigration so, yes, it is orderly and it is fair and it is legal, but it continues to welcome strivers and dreamers from all around the world. That's why I'm a Democrat, that's the set of ideas that I believe in.

Oh, I am here to tell you that even if you don't agree with me or Democrats on policy, even if you believe in more Libertarian economic theories, even if you are an evangelical and our position on certain social issues is a bridge too far, even if you think my assessment of immigration is mistaken and that Democrats aren't serious enough about immigration enforcement, I'm here to tell you that you should still be concerned with our current course and should still want to see a restoration of honesty and decency and lawfulness in our government.

It should not be Democratic or Republican, it should not be a partisan issue to say that we do not pressure the Attorney General or the FBI to use the criminal justice system as a cudgel to punish our political opponents.

Or to explicitly call on the Attorney General to protect members of our own party from prosecution because an election happens to be coming up. I'm not making that up. That's not hypothetical. It shouldn't be Democratic or Republican to say that we don't threaten the freedom of the press because -- they say things or publish stories we don't like.

I complained plenty about Fox News -- but you never heard me threaten to shut them down, or call them enemies of the people. It shouldn't be Democratic or Republican to say we don't target certain groups of people based on what they look like or how they pray. We are Americans. We're supposed to standup to bullies.

Not follow them.

We're supposed to stand up to discrimination. And we're sure as heck supposed to stand up, clearly and unequivocally, to Nazi sympathizers.

How hard can that be? Saying that Nazis are bad. I'll be honest, sometimes I get into arguments with progressive friends about what the current political movement requires. There are well-meaning folks passionate about social justice, who think things have gotten so bad, the lines have been so starkly drawn, that we have to fight fire with fire, we have to do the same things to the Republicans that they do to us, adopt their tactics, say whatever works, make up stuff about the other side.

I don't agree with that. It's not because I'm soft. It's not because I'm interested in promoting an empty bipartisanship. I don't agree with it because eroding our civic institutions and our civic trust and making people angrier and yelling at each other and making people cynical about government, that always works better for those who don't believe in the power of collective action.

You don't need an effective government or a robust press or reasoned debate to work when all you're concerned about is maintaining power. In fact, the more cynical people are about government and the angrier and more dispirited they are about the prospects for change, the more likely the powerful are able to maintain their power. But we believe that in order to move this country forward, to actually solve problems and make people's lives better, we need a well-functioning government, we need our civic institutions to work.

We need cooperation among people of different political persuasions. And to make that work, we have to restore our faith in democracy. We have to bring people together, not tear them apart. We need majorities in Congress and state legislatures who are serious about governing and want to bring about real change and improvements in people's lives.

And we won't win people over by calling them names, or dismissing entire chunks of the country as racist, or sexist, or homophobic. When I say bring people together, I mean all of our people. You know, this whole notion that has sprung up recently about Democrats need to choose between trying to appeal to the white working class voters, or voters of color, and women and LGBT Americans, that's nonsense. I don't buy that. I got votes from every demographic.

We won by reaching out to everybody and competing everywhere and by fighting for every vote. And that's what we've got to do in this election and every election after that.

And we can't do that if we immediately disregard what others have to say from the start because they're not like us, because they're not -- because they're white or they're black or they're men or women, or they're gay or they're straight; if we think that somehow there's no way they can understand how I'm feeling, and therefore don't have any standing to speak on certain matters because we're only defined by certain characteristics.

That doesn't work if you want a healthy democracy. We can't do that if we traffic in absolutes when it comes to policy. You know, to make democracy work we have to be able to get inside the reality of people who are different, have different experiences, come from different backgrounds. We have to engage them even when it is frustrating; we have to listen to them even when we don't like what they have to say; we have to hope that we can change their minds and we have to remain open to them changing ours.

And that doesn't mean, by the way, abandoning our principles or caving to bad policy in the interests of maintaining some phony version of "civility." That seems to be, by the way, the definition of civility offered by too many Republicans right now: We will be polite as long as we get a hundred percent of what we want and you don't callus out on the various ways that we're sticking it to people. And we'll click our tongues and issue vague statements of disappointment when the President does something outrageous, but we won't actually do anything about it. That's not civility. That's abdicating your responsibilities.

But again I digress. Making democracy work means holding on to our principles, having clarity about our principles, and then having the confidence to get in the arena and have a serious debate. And it also means appreciating that progress does not happen all at once, but when you put your shoulder to the wheel, if you're willing to fight for it, things do get better.

And let me tell you something, particularly young people here. Better is good. I used to have to tell my young staff this all the time in the White House. Better is good. That's the history of progress in this country. Not perfect. Better. The Civil Rights Act didn't end racism, but it made things better. Social Security didn't eliminate all poverty for seniors, but it made things better for millions of people.

Do not let people tell you the fight's not worth it because you won't get everything that you want. The idea that, well, you know there's racism in America so I'm not going to bother voting. No point. That makes no sense. You can make it better. Better's always worth fighting for. That's how our founders expected this system of self-government to work; that through the testing of ideas and the application of reason and evidence and proof, we could sort through our differences and nobody would get exactly what they wanted, but it would be possible to find a basis for common ground.

And that common ground exists. Maybe it's not fashionable to say that right now. It's hard to see it with all the nonsense in Washington, it's hard to hear it with all the noise. But common ground exists. I have seen it. I have lived it. I know there are white people who care deeply about black people being treated unfairly. I have talked to them and loved them. And I know there are black people who care deeply about the struggles of white rural America. I'm one of them and I have a track record to prove it

I know there are evangelicals who are deeply committed to doing something about climate change. I've seen them do the work. I know there are conservatives who think there's nothing compassionate about separating immigrant children from their mothers. I know there are Republicans who believe government should only perform a few minimal functions but that one of those functions should be making sure nearly 3,000 Americans don't die in a hurricane and its aftermath.

Common ground's out there. I see it every day. Just how people interact, how people treat each other. You see it on the ball field. You see it at work. You see it in places of worship.

But to say that a common ground exists doesn't mean it will inevitably win out. History shows the power of fear. And the closer that we get to Election Day, the more those invested in the politics of fear and division will work, will do anything to hang on to their recent gains.

Fortunately I am hopeful because out of this political darkness I am seeing a great awakening of citizenship all across the country. I cannot tell you how encouraged I've been by watching so many people get involved for the first time, or the first time in a long time. They're marching and they're organizing and they're registering people to vote, and they're running for office themselves. Look at this crop of Democratic candidates running for Congress and running for governor, running for the state legislature, running for district attorney, running for school board. It is a movement of citizens who happen to be younger and more diverse and more female than ever before, and that's really useful.

We need more women in charge. But we've got first-time candidates, we've got veterans of Iraq and Afghanistan, record numbers of women -- Americans who previously maybe didn't have an interest in politics as a career, but laced up their shoes and rolled up their sleeves and grabbed a clipboard because they too believe, this time's different; this moment's too important to sit out. And if you listen to what these candidates are talking about, in individual races across the country, you'll find they're not just running against something, they are running for something. They're running to expand opportunity and they're running to restore the honor and compassion that should be the essence of public service.

And speaking as a Democrat, that's when the Democratic Party has always made the biggest difference in the lives of the American people, when we led with conviction and principle and bold new ideas. The antidote to a government controlled by a powerful fear, a government that divides, is a government by the organized, energized, inclusive many. That's what this moment's about. That has to be the answer.

You cannot sit back and wait for a saviour. You can't opt out because you don't feel sufficiently inspired by this or that particular candidate. This is not a rock concert, this is not Coachella. You don't need a messiah. All we need are decent, honest, hardworking people who are accountable -- and who have America's best interests at heart.

And they'll step up and they'll join our government and they will make things better if they have support. One election will not fix everything that needs to be fixed, but it will be a start. And you have to start it. What's going to fix our democracy is you.

People ask me, what are you going to do for the election? No, the question is: What are you going to do? You're the antidote. Your participation and your spirit and your determination, not just in this election but in every subsequent election, and in the days between elections.

Because in the end, the threat to our democracy doesn't just come from Donald Trump or the current batch of Republicans in Congress or the Koch Brothers and their lobbyists, or too much compromise from Democrats, or Russian hacking. The biggest threat to our democracy is indifference. The biggest threat to our democracy is cynicism – a cynicism that's led too many people to turn away from politics and stay home on Election Day.

To all the young people who are here today, there are now more eligible voters in your generation than in any other, which means your generation now has more power than anybody to change things. If you want it, you can make sure America gets out of its current funk. If you actually care about it, you have the power to make sure we seize a brighter future. But to exercise that clout, to exercise that power, you have to show up.

In the last midterms election, in, fewer than one in five young people voted. One in five. Not two in five, or three in five. One in five. Is it any wonder this Congress doesn't reflect your values and your priorities? Are you surprised by that?

This whole project of self- government only works if everybody's doing their part. Don't tell me your vote doesn't matter. I've won states in the presidential election because of five, ten, twenty votes per precinct. And if you thought elections don't matter, I hope these last two years have corrected that impression.

So if you don't like what's going on right now -- and you shouldn't -- do not complain. Don't hashtag. Don't get anxious. Don't retreat. Don't binge on whatever it is you're bingeing on. Don't lose yourself in ironic detachment. Don't put your head in the sand. Don't boo. Vote.

Vote. If you are really concerned about how the

criminal justice system treats African-Americans, the best way to protest is to vote -- not just for Senators and Representatives, but for mayors and sheriffs and state legislators. Do what they just did in Philadelphia and Boston, and elect state's attorneys and district attorneys who are looking at issues in a new light, who realize that the vast majority of law enforcement do the right thing in a really hard job, and we just need to make sure that all of them do.

If you're tired of politicians who offer nothing but "thoughts and prayers" after a mass shooting, you've got to do what the Parkland kids are doing. Some of them aren't even eligible to vote, yet they're out there working to change minds and registering people, and they're not giving up until we have a Congress that sees your lives as more important than a campaign check from the NRA.

You've got to vote. If you support the MeToo movement, you're outraged by stories of sexual harassment and assault inspired by the women who shared them, you've got to do more than retweet a hashtag. You've got to vote.

Part of the reason women are more vulnerable in the workplace is because not enough women are bosses in the workplace -- which is why we need to strengthen and enforce laws that protect women in the workplace not just from harassment but from discrimination in hiring and promotion, and not getting paid the same amount for doing the same work. That requires laws. Laws get passed by legislators.

You've got to vote. When you vote, you've got the power to make it easier to afford college, and harder to shoot up a school. When you vote, you've got the power to make sure a family keeps its health insurance; you could save somebody's life. When you vote, you've got the power to make sure white nationalists don't feel emboldened to march with their hoods off or their hoods on in Charlottesville in the middle of the day.

Thirty minutes. Thirty minutes of your time. Is democracy worth that? We have been through much darker times than these, and somehow each generation of Americans carried us through to the other side. Not by sitting around and waiting for something to happen, not by leaving it to others to do something, but by leading that movement for change themselves.

And if you do that, if you get involved, and you get engaged, and you knock on some doors, and you talk with your friends, and you argue with your family members, and you change some minds, and you vote, something powerful happens.

Change happens. Hope happens. Not perfection. Not every bit of cruelty and sadness and poverty and disease suddenly stricken from the earth. There will still be problems. But with each new candidate that surprises you with a victory that you supported, a spark of hope happens.

With each new law that helps a kid read or helps a homeless family find shelter or helps a veteran get the support he or she has earned, each time that happens, hope happens. With each new step we take in the direction of fairness and justice and equality and opportunity, hope spreads.

And that can be the legacy of your generation. You can be the generation that at a critical moment stood up and reminded us just how precious this experiment in democracy really is, just how powerful it can be when we fight for it, when we believe in it.

I believe in you. I believe you will help lead us in the right direction. And I will be right there with you every step of the way.

Thank you, Illinois. God bless. God bless this country we love. Thank you.

Préface

2025. Une année au bord de l'abîme, un croisement imprévisible où s'entrelacent espoir et désespoir, innovation et destruction, résilience et effondrement. Cet ouvrage n'est pas une prophétie, mais une réflexion audacieuse sur les possibles de demain.

Lorsque nous tentons de deviner l'avenir, nous ne faisons jamais que tendre un miroir aux incertitudes de notre présent. À travers ces pages, j'ai cherché à explorer les dynamiques qui façonnent notre monde : les crises globales qui grondent, les bouleversements technologiques qui réinventent nos existences, et les forces spirituelles, sociales et philosophiques qui nous poussent à chercher un sens dans le chaos. Mais, soyons clairs : **les scénarios présentés ici ne sont ni des certitudes ni des faits avérés. Ce sont des constructions hypothétiques, des exercices de projection dans un futur incertain.**

Pourquoi ce besoin d'explorer l'inconnu ? Parce que l'humanité se trouve face à un dilemme existentiel. Nous naviguons sur une mer tourmentée, sans carte précise, mais avec une boussole : notre capacité à réfléchir, à choisir et à agir. Les scénarios décrits à la fin de cet ouvrage – résilience proactive, chaos maîtrisé, fragmentation ou transformation radicale – ne sont pas des prédictions. Ce sont des cadres de pensée, des possibilités offertes à notre imagination et à notre volonté collective.

La puissance des mots réside dans leur capacité à éveiller les consciences, à provoquer des débats, et, parfois, à inspirer des actions. Cet ouvrage ne prétend pas avoir toutes les réponses. Il ne dicte pas une vérité, mais offre des pistes, des réflexions et, espérons-le, des élans pour imaginer un avenir qui, malgré les ombres, demeure à écrire.

En refermant ce livre, souvenez-vous : ce que nous avons dressé ici, ce sont des possibles, des reflets d'un présent tourmenté. L'avenir appartient à ceux qui sauront le modeler avec lucidité, courage et humanité.

Bonne lecture, et surtout, gardez l'espoir.
Nous sommes les écrivains de demain.

Nicolas Z. Gassié
Décembre 2024